MEAN DADS

FOR A BETTER AMERICA

MEAN DADS

FOR A
BETTER AMERICA

THE GENEROUS REWARDS OF
AN OLD-FASHIONED CHILDHOOD

TOM SHILLUE

DEY ST.
An Imprint of WILLIAM MORROW

MEAN DADS FOR A BETTER AMERICA. Copyright © 2017 by Tom Shillue Productions, Inc. All rights reserved. Printed in the United States of America. No part of this book may be used or reproduced in any manner whatsoever without written permission except in the case of brief quotations embodied in critical articles and reviews. For information, address HarperCollins Publishers, 195 Broadway, New York, NY 10007.

HarperCollins books may be purchased for educational, business, or sales promotional use. For information, please email the Special Markets Department at SPsales@harpercollins.com.

FIRST EDITION

Designed by Suet Yee Chong

Library of Congress Cataloging-in-Publication Data has been applied for.

ISBN 978-0-06-265617-9

17 18 19 20 21   DIX/LSC   10 9 8 7 6 5 4 3 2 1

For Denise, Agnes, and Louise

CONTENTS

INTRODUCTION   1

CHAPTER 1 **BE AFRAID**   9

CHAPTER 2 **BE PRACTICAL**   19

CHAPTER 3 **BE SATISFIED**   25

CHAPTER 4 **BE THRIFTY**   39

CHAPTER 5 **BE COMPETITIVE**   51

CHAPTER 6 **BE CONFIDENT**   63

CHAPTER 7 **BE CREATIVE**   77

CHAPTER 8 **BE DEDICATED**   85

CHAPTER 9 **BE RECKLESS**   95

CHAPTER 10 **BE PREPARED**   103

CHAPTER 11 **BE REVERENT**   113

CHAPTER 12 **BE A GENTLEMAN**   123

CHAPTER 13 **BE YOURSELF**   133

CHAPTER 14 **BE BOLD**   141

CHAPTER 15 **BE OPEN-MINDED**   149

CHAPTER 16 **BE(AT) IT**   157

CHAPTER 17 **BE ROGUE** 161

CHAPTER 18 **BE NEW WAVE** 171

CHAPTER 19 **BE SUPPORTIVE** 185

CHAPTER 20 **BE A (SLIGHTLY NAÏVE) JOKER** 201

CHAPTER 21 **B♭ MINOR** 217

CHAPTER 22 **BE PROUD** 247

CHAPTER 23 **BE GRATEFUL** 255

ACKNOWLEDGMENTS 271

INTRODUCTION

WHEN I MARCHED OFF TO MY FIRST DAY OF kindergarten in September of 1971, I had no idea where my school was. "Just walk in the same direction as all the other kids!" my mother yelled to me from the porch, and off I went. I quickly found a pack of kids about my size moving along with their lunch boxes and I joined them. We all wandered along together like cattle, and eventually ended up at school.

I have such strong memories of my childhood during that time. Whenever you see a movie or TV show that's set in the late 1960s or early '70s, everyone's decked out in headbands, beaded vests, and bell-bottoms like they just left the Woodstock Festival and are on their way to a Vietnam War protest, but that's not what most of the world looked like. I grew up in the town of Norwood, Massachusetts, and like 99 percent of the country at that time, it was a lot closer to Mayberry, with dads that looked like Andy Griffith and kids that looked like Opie.

On July Fourth and Memorial Day the Shillues would go down to the center of town and watch the veterans march, followed by the Colonial Boys playing in the fife and drum corps in the yearly parades. We waved American flags and saluted the soldiers as they walked by, and although there may have been protests about all kinds of things happening on faraway college campuses, we didn't hear much about them. It was still Cold War America, the U.S.S.R. versus the U.S.A., and we knew who the good guys were.

The secret to my happy childhood, I believe, was in the contrasts. I think my family was the only one in Massachusetts driving around in a Volkswagen bus with a Nixon/Agnew sticker on the bumper. We were surrounded by the art and music of the peace movement, the mainstream stuff anyway: the Kingston Trio, Simon and Garfunkel, the Beatles, and Three Dog Night played from our hi-fi in the living room, and there were Peter Max posters in our bedrooms and peace signs decorating our refrigerator. But, somehow, my mother managed to embrace the hippie aesthetic of the 1970s without succumbing to its worldview. So when we were piling out of the Volkswagen looking like a gang from a collectivist commune, we were headed into St. Catherine's church together.

In many ways, this meant we got the best of both worlds. My childhood was like the Bing Crosby movie *The Bells of St. Mary's*, set to the soundtrack from the musical *Godspell*. It was Freedom, Love, Peace, and Fierce Individuality, all mixed up with Parental Authority, Moral Absolutism, and Fear of God. A rich, hearty recipe for happiness if ever there was one.

The TV we consumed was mostly syndicated reruns from

the '50s and '60s. We watched *The Rifleman, My Three Sons, Andy Griffith,* and *Dragnet,* shows with moral codes matching their black and white palettes. The Boy Scout manual I used as a kid was an old hand-me-down from my uncle, but its contents matched the curriculum my troop followed: the same exercises, the same merit badges, the same Scouts honor. Why did I need a new one? The ideals in it were enduring. There was also no talking back or "positive discipline" then. There was no hugging it out or sharing our feelings or family meetings. You did what you were told as a kid and then you got to have fun. A+B = C, or something like that.

I think the decade of the 1970s was probably the greatest time ever to be a kid, but only if it came with the teaspoon of castor oil that was 1950s America. There were many tumultuous issues of the day—Watergate, the Vietnam War, gas shortages, birth control, the ERA; these issues weren't for kids, though. They were simmering in the background. In the foreground were Church, God, Country, baseball, hot dogs, apple pie, Chevrolet, parades, heroes, and the Red, White and Blue.

I might have grown up in the '70s but I was raised *by the '50s*.

Things started to change when I became a teenager, as they usually do. I know this because when I was in high school in the 1980s I kept a diary beside my bed. It wasn't my idea—I'd gotten it from a pro football player who had come to speak at one of my high school assemblies. During a Q&A session, he was asked if he had any advice for young people, and he said, "Keep a diary. It doesn't matter what you write in it, just do it. Try to write something every day. Otherwise you'll forget everything from this part of your life."

Well, that was all I needed. Diaries had always seemed like kind of a girl thing, but since the recommendation had come from a football player, I went right out and bought a blank, unlined book and began filling it. Such is the power of male role models. And the football player was absolutely right. My memory from my high school years is no match for the vivid recall I have from my youngest days, so without the diary I don't think I would remember half of that time.*

I recently opened mine up, and it was quite enlightening, as well as a little embarrassing—it's quite heavy on the words *I*, *me*, and *myself*.

Here was an entry titled "self-evaluation":

I, like many other people constantly wonder what other people think of me. I'm an extrovert. This means I'm very sociable, very outspoken, and even loud sometimes.

In fact, I often wonder how some people get through life without much attention at all. If I tried to go a day without purposely calling attention to myself, I would find it difficult.

I probably should have titled it "self-absorption," but nevertheless my analysis was spot on. It was 1984 and MTV was new; I was embracing the new wave music scene and doing everything I could to draw attention to myself at school. I was listening to the B-52's and DEVO, and I colored my hair David Bowie-red with henna, and dressed like a Discount Duran Duran. (It all seems very mainstream now, but believe me, in the New England suburbs where "Zeppelin Rules!"

---

* I can't remember the football player's name because I didn't have a diary yet. There's more evidence for any young person reading this—keep a diary! And Snapchat doesn't count.

that was enough to get you labeled a "Wicked Weeid-oh!") To be honest, I was treating my high school life as a performance and trying to establish myself as different, unique, avant-garde. Having grown up conservative and straight-laced, I was clearly seeking to spread my wings and try out a new persona. And you can tell from my diary, I relished my status as an outsider.

> *I wonder however about my nonconformity. I try my utmost to nonconform to anything—groups at school, Mom and Dad's expectations, the entire country in general. I honestly don't know how I will feel about certain things until I find out about how the masses feel.*
>
> *Then I almost always take the other side. If there is a conservative versus liberal argument, I take the liberal. I love being a liberal . . .*

I'm so glad that I have this down in print. None of my adult friends would believe it otherwise. There is an old saying that if you're not a liberal when you're twenty, you have no heart and if you're not a conservative when you're forty, you have no brain. Well, I'm living proof. I don't think anyone who watches me on Foxs News Channel would say I "take the liberal" side about anything at all. While my commentary doesn't usually involve deep policy discussions, I'm more likely to take the "traditional" side on any issue. Some viewers may be inclined to describe me as "charmingly old-fashioned," while others may opt for "anachronistic and regressive." I'm just fine with this.

My teenage progressivism would manifest itself in passionate lunchroom discussions and afterschool arguments about tolerance and open-mindedness, in which I always took the side of the underdog. I rarely "won" these arguments, but I always found a way to throw in a quote from *Jonathan Livingston Seagull* or *Zen and the Art of Motorcycle Maintenance* (my two deep-thought standbys). But I think I developed my love of liberalism for mostly practical reasons:

> *I love being a liberal . . . and arguing on the left, because it is always so idealistic and humanistic, that you can broaden your argument to ideals, while the conservative must stick to the issue at hand. For example, with a nuclear debate, the conservative must take a definite stance—"the Russians are bad guys, we must protect ourselves against them, we need missiles for security." * The liberal can stray from the topic all he wants—"Look, we're all human beings. Look what we're doing to each other. Neither of us wants war, so why don't we just disarm?" You see? Both views are right, and the liberal will understand the leftist approach, the conservative the right-wing approach.*
>
> *I believe that liberalism is fundamentally correct while conservatism is more practical in our society. If everyone were a liberal, the world would be a nice place. If everyone were a conservative, the world would be a very orderly, unfriendly place, kind of like a business. But as it is, the world is very interesting and argumentative. I've strayed from the topic of self-evaluation. I'll continue later.*

The attention span of a high school student being what it is, I never did continue the topic later as promised. So, perhaps

---

* We really did talk about the Russians all the time back then. There is always one overriding liberal versus conservative argument going on in our culture. Now it seems to be Global Warming, in the '80s it was Nuclear Disarmament.

it's time! All this looking back got me thinking about how I got here. How did I go from small-town radical to big-city conservative? Was I able to hold on to my heart *and* keep my brain? Well, if I did, I'm pretty sure it has to do with how I was raised. So why don't we start from the beginning?

CHAPTER 1
BE AFRAID

N MOST SATURDAY MORNINGS, MY BROTHER BILLY and I would wake to my dad's voice: "GET IN THE CAH."

It was Darth Vader with a Boston Accent. The tone, the breathing, the dramatic pause, followed by the sudden sweeping exit. My dad didn't need the helmet and cape, he had the attitude. He was six feet tall, average height, but seemed like a giant to us. He had the same weathered Irish American looks that most other dads in Norwood, Massachusetts, had, but he had an extra, brooding intensity. The kind that comes in handy when you're leading a Galactic Empire through fear and intimidation, or trying to get two young boys to wake up early on a weekend morning and get in the car.

Billy and I would immediately scramble downstairs and get into the back seat of Dad's Dodge Dart. Back then seat belts were optional, by law and by custom. Even if you did get those lap belts on, they fit pretty loosely, so if your dad took a left, you went sliding all the way over to the right; then when he took a right, you slid back to the middle. We felt perfectly safe, even though we probably wouldn't have survived a minor accident. My dad would drive in silence, always leaving us to wonder where we might be going. We were never told, and we knew better than to ask. We wondered, *Would it be to the site of the Boston Massacre? A walk on the deck of* Old Ironsides? *A climb up the steeple of the Old North Church? Perhaps a stroll along the Freedom Trail?*

Clearly, our excursions tended to involve the Revolutionary War, but it wasn't because my dad was some kind of colonial buff. We lived in New England in 1976, and everyone was stricken with Bicentennial fever. It seemed that we had been celebrating this event for my whole childhood, actually: every town was preparing for its own Bicentennial celebration, and in school we would perform Bicentennial plays, sing Bicentennial songs, and paint Bicentennial dinner plates. I heard the word almost daily, but I was unclear on what it actually meant. To me, it was just synonymous with *Revolutionary War.*

One day in our third-grade class our teacher, Miss Barnacle, asked Brian Ridikas, "In what war did the minutemen fight?" and he answered, "The Bicentennial." As everyone laughed and Miss Barnacle scolded him for his ignorance, I remember thinking that I might have given the same answer.

On those Saturday trips with Dad, Billy and I always enjoyed whatever historical exhibit we visited, but getting there was a challenge. Carsickness ran deep in our family. My mother did not believe in drug therapy for this condition; she believed that the main cause of motion sickness was the presence of too much visual stimuli. Her solution was to simply make us all wear sunglasses in the car, so she kept many of her old pairs in great supply in the glove compartment. She would pass them out and instruct each of us to put them on whenever we traveled, which was supposed to keep us from looking out the windows and getting dizzy. I'm not sure how well this worked, but if we ever did complain of nausea, my mother would never blame her remedy. She always blamed our behavior. "Sit still and let the glasses do their work!" she would scream. When the car would stop at a rest area, all of us would pile out gasping for air and dripping in cold sweat, but all wearing oversized ladies' sunglasses. We must have looked like we were in the witness protection program.

Complaining was *really* not an option when traveling with my dad, so my brother and I would try to sit still in the back seat and grind out the nausea as best we could. It didn't help that we were always hungry, probably because we had been woken up Vader-style before dawn. Despite the fact that our stomachs were technically empty, we always had something down there from dinner the night before that we could manage to throw up. There would be no warning. My dad would be driving along, deep in thought, as Billy and I in the back seat were slowly turning yellow in the face. All of a sudden, there was a splashing sound on the floor mats.

He would silently pull over to the side of the road, and we'd all get out to assess the damage. My brother or I would shake off our clothes as best we could (the rest would dry and fall off on the way up Bunker Hill), while my dad would take handfuls of dirt from the roadside and shake it over the mess on the floor mats, covering it with a layer of dust. Of course, none of this masked the smell; it just turned the wet vomit into dirty vomit. But it was a good try—real American ingenuity at work.

Throwing up was like rebooting the system, so at least the carsickness passed after that. As my dad drove on, Billy and I were faced with a new dilemma—finding ways to suppress our growing hunger.

Our greatest desire on any of these sightseeing day trips was to stop at a McDonald's. You did have to actually stop and go *into* the McDonald's, as these were pre-drive-thru days, (which was a good thing considering the vomit-covered floor mats).

We would pass one every ten minutes or so thinking, *would this be the one?* As a Golden Arches sign approached, we'd stare straight ahead, following it with our peripheral vision, and pray. We'd attempt to control the car's movement with our minds: *Pull into the driveway . . . take a right into the parking lot. . . . Pull in right . . . now!* Most times our car would drive right by. But on those rare occasions that my dad did pull into a McDonald's, did we scream with pure delight? Oh no, we reacted with complete indifference. Our expressions didn't change at all.

My dad would break the silence, "You boys hungry?"

"Mmmm . . . I don't know," Billy would say, casually. "I guess so."

"Uh . . . maybe . . . OK," I'd add without emotion.

It was an unwritten rule between us: that showing our true excitement for McDonald's would lessen the chance of future visits. Not only was it unwritten, it was unfounded; based on nothing that my dad ever said, but on our assumption of our dad's overriding philosophy: "Expect nothing, because you deserve nothing." It existed entirely in our heads. I've recently confirmed this with my brother. My father never once actually expressed this philosophy, but we believed it wholeheartedly, especially in regards to McDonald's. We never once spoke to each other about this in our childhood, but we both instinctively had strong feelings about the McDonald's rule, and acted accordingly. We probably thought we were pulling one over on my dad with our casual routine, but I'm sure that even the least perceptive adult could have guessed our real feelings once we got our food. We tore through the paper covering on those hamburgers like a couple of raccoons.

The reason it was usually just me and my brother with my dad was that on Saturdays, my parents split up us kids; Mom took the girls and Dad took the boys. Kathy was the oldest, and the most serious, as the oldest tends to be. Ann was a little wilder, prone to singing at the top of her lungs whether anyone wanted to hear her or not. During my childhood she was the second oldest kid, now she's a few years younger than me (that does happen). Next was my brother, who had a mind for the mathematical, the rational, and the statistical—he was everything I was not. I've often remarked that if he and I were combined into one, we would make a pretty impressive man. As I was the youngest (for the first six years of my life, anyway), both girls considered me their plaything, and would dress me up and parade me around the house in costume for laughs—my very first performances. Mary Ellen was the last to arrive, a late addition to our family for sure, but probably just in time for me, relieving me from the terrible burden of being the cutest thing in the house.

But back in the early days, Saturdays meant two girls with Mom and two boys with Dad. It was probably never planned that way; chances are one morning my dad just said "Get in the cah" to my brother and me and a tradition was born. I don't really even know what Mom and the girls did, but I'm sure it had to do with The Bicentennial.

I do recall one special day when it was all of us; my two sisters, my brother, and me. There we were in the Volkswagen with my parents, on the way home after a long day trip to the New England Boat show. My dad took us to many of these boat shows. Year after year he would take us to the convention center and we'd follow him as he walked the aisles, stroking his chin and trying to decide if he should take the plunge. For him I think all the fun was in the shopping. He did eventually buy a twenty-foot sailboat (not at a boat show—he got it used through the want ads like a real man) and kept it moored in Boston Harbor for a few years, but if you added up all the time he spent on the water, it would not even come close to the time he spent shopping for it.

On the drive back from the boat show, my brother and I, famished from a long day of staring at fiberglass hulls, were doing our usual routine of sitting in silence and praying to the Lord above that my dad would pull into the world's finest eatery, when suddenly my sister Ann yelled out, "I want Mc-Donald's! Let's go to McDonald's!"

My brother and I looked at each other, stunned. She had broken the rule! What was she thinking! We knew there would be grave consequences in the next few moments: not only would we not be eating hamburgers that day, we may never go to McDonald's again. She had ruined it for all of us. How could she be so foolish? We prepared ourselves for the worst.

Then my father did something quite shocking.

"OK," he said, pulling into the McDonald's parking lot.

Both my sisters cheered. Billy and I remained silent. That was all it took? We could have just *asked*? This revelation shook us to the core. It seemed too easy. However, after some thought we determined that it was a fluke; it would never work out that easily for us. Ann had obviously taken advantage of some daughter loophole, but we would surely end up paying for her hubris. Although her unorthodox "ask" method had gotten us to McDonald's that day, surely that method would not apply to sons, whose motto, as you know, is "Be brave, be silent, be hungry."

We were never bold enough to even test my sister's approach. The following Saturday, Billy and I got in the car as usual and resumed with our usual "silent prayer" method. This was the way it was meant to be. The rule, even if it was based on nothing, would hold. Why tinker with an occasionally successful method when the alternative required doing the thing we most wanted to avoid when it came to our father: speaking up?

Some might wonder why my brother and I were so afraid to ask our father for anything. The reason is simple: dads were meaner in the 1970s. Back then, fearing your dad was what you did. That's why so many guys of my generation had such an attachment to *Star Wars*. We all remember that dramatic scene in *The Empire Strikes Back*, and the deep, chilling voice of Darth Vader as he confronts young Luke Skywalker: "Luke, I am your father!"

Boys like me everywhere were sitting in the movie theater clutching their popcorn bucket thinking, *Yeah that makes perfect sense . . . I can't believe I didn't see that one coming!*

As much as the world was changing in the 1970s, the world inside our home was much like the America of decades past, or centuries, even. Think about it: our country was about to have its two-hundredth birthday, and I'll bet my dad wasn't much different from George Washington's dad: stoic, stern, and authoritarian. But George Washington turned out okay, and we would, too.

I understand that I had a great and fortunate childhood. I was not the victim of strict parenting, but a beneficiary of it. When someone hears me say "Mean Dads," they might think, *But my dad was mean and he ruined my life!* But that's a different story. Of course, real abuse is a tragedy, but what passes as "mean" today used to just be called "parenting."

I spent much of my childhood in fear. Fear of God, fear of my parents, fear of the other adults in the neighborhood, fear of bullying kids. But fear is not always a bad thing—it keeps you alive. Fearing actual danger is very important. As you grow up you learn which fears are real and which are not, and it's always liberating to discover when one of your fears is unfounded. You think, *My dad is going to kill me when he finds out!* But then he doesn't kill you. You live to see another day. Your dad is not a murderer—that's great news to a kid!

Then you realize, *Perhaps he wants me to* think *that he is going to kill me, so next time I'll think twice before starting a fire in the garage.* Dad worked in mysterious ways, like someone else I know. Fearing God is obviously important, but how are you going to fear God if you don't fear your dad? He's not God, but for a while he's a pretty good stand-in.

I think my dad belonged to what was truly the last era for scary dads, and even he caught the tail end of it. You can bet his dad was even scarier than him, and his dad before that. The further back you go, the scarier they were. If you doubt that, just look at any family photograph from the turn of the last century, and ask yourself if the wife and children look anything but terrified of the man in the mustache and derby hat standing beside them. When I look at one of those pictures, I always think, *Is that his family, or is he holding them hostage?*

I don't need to be like that guy, but I wouldn't mind if my kids were a *little bit* afraid of me. I mean, throw a dad a bone, modern world—and not for my sake, for theirs. Because if I could be a Darth Vader dad, I'd use the dark side for good. At least that's what I tell myself, as I look up at the stars, and noisily breathe in and out.

CHAPTER 2

BE PRACTICAL

WHEN I WAS VERY YOUNG, MY MOTHER USED TO tie me to a tree in the backyard. That way, I could play outside and she didn't have to worry about where I'd wander off to. She could get her housework done and I could experience the great outdoors—a win-win, as it were. Today, of course, if you search the Internet for the phrase "child tied to tree," you'll see all sorts of news stories that end with some version of the phrase "mother arrested for child abuse." But that was not my story—the way my mother tells it, I loved that rope and harness. The rope allowed me to run around in a fifteen-foot circumference like a dog. I usually stayed taut at the end of the line, but sometimes I would run around and around, eventually coiling myself tightly against the trunk of the tree. I'm lucky there were no large birds of prey in Massachusetts; with the rope strung tightly around my plump flesh

I probably looked delicious. After some time, a kind passerby would happen upon me stuck to the tree and help me unwind. Basically, if all my older siblings were off at school, I was on my own. Babysitters were only for emergencies, and "Nanny" was what we called my grandmother, who came just once a week so my mother could go grocery shopping (which was an all-day affair because my mom was a founding member of what I call the "militant couponing community").

One day, when I was three, my mother decided to let me off the leash. Her only instruction: "Do not go in the street." For a while, I stayed in the half-moon-shaped trench I had worn out in front of the tree when tied on my tether, where I felt most at home. Then at some point I got courageous and broke out on my own, completely forgetting my mother's orders.

My mother emerged from the house when she heard a car horn honking, and saw me sitting in the middle of the street, a big Chrysler stopped in front of me, the driver leaning out the window making a "Shoo!" gesture with his hands. It may seem callous now, but back then the driver's behavior was entirely unremarkable. It was 1969 after all, and at that time children were mostly seen as pests, not America's most precious resource. As my mother tells it, I got up from the pavement upon seeing her, walked up to the porch where she was standing arms akimbo in the doorway, and passed by her and into the house without a sound. I returned moments later with my head hanging low and the rope and harness in my outstretched hand.

My mother loves to tell this story, ending with the image: the chastened boy who knew he was fated to be returned to his place at the tree. But as a parent now, I think the more illuminating part of the story comes a bit earlier. In taking me off the leash, my mother was willing to roll the dice and see if I lived to tell the tale. I did live, and in giving me that leeway, she allowed me to learn a valuable lesson: I would never again wander into the street. I ask you, what modern parent would take a risk like that today? Let's just make an educated guess and round it out at "none."

But what if the experiment had not ended well? What if my mother had stepped outside to find me laid out on the road with a Michelin tire tread across my forehead? Well, she had five kids, and the other four would have certainly learned from my mistake. You can bet that at my funeral, as my little casket was being lowered into the earth, my mother would have turned to my brothers and sisters and said, "See what happens when you go out in the street?"

We needed tough lessons like this as children of that time because we had to be tough. An occasional playground fight was expected as the norm, and if we complained to our mother that we were being teased, we were treated to this glorious aphorism: "Sticks and stones may break my bones, but names will never hurt me." My mom used to say that all the time, one of the seemingly endless adages she had at her disposal to deal with any of life's problems. To this day I think long and hard about the practical application that dogma had on my life.

The idea that you could actually choose whether or not to be hurt by words: that was huge for me. Even though it has been repeated ad nauseam for generations, "sticks and stones" really is a powerful bit of philosophy to a kid. That's one of the great things about being a parent: you can spout nothing but clichés, and yet, to your child, you come off as one of the great thinkers in Western culture.

That's true, I thought. *If someone punches you in the chest, it hurts no matter what. But with words, it all depends on how you think about it. Mom's a genius!*

I look at the rough and tumble world of childhood and the process of learning to deal with bullying and being insulted as a form of inoculation. After each instance of being offended and repeating my mother's "sticks and stones" philosophy in my head, I eventually created a vaccine that built up my immune system.

A few years later, when I was off the leash and was able to venture out into the neighborhood, there was a period when I was afraid to go outside. Chrissy Sullivan across the street, who was a little younger than me but unfortunately a little bigger, would push me around whenever he saw me. So, I would stand by the window in our living room and make sure he wasn't out and about before I ventured outside. My mother took notice and gave me that advice that mothers have relied on for generations.

"What are you worried about?" she asked.

"That big kid always beats me up," I said.

"So what? He's not so big—just hit him back! Give him a good punch, and he won't bother you anymore."

Although I didn't exactly welcome her advice, she'd been right about the "names will never hurt me" part, so I figured she knew what she was talking about. I went outside, and sure enough, the minute Chrissy spotted me he crossed the street and started shoving me. So I wound up and punched him right in the stomach. I must have really knocked the wind out of him because he looked completely shocked and began to back away. Then he sucked in a deep breath, turned, and ran. I probably should have left it at that and just yelled something like "And there's more where that came from!" Instead I ran after him and chased him back to his house. He darted up on the porch and tried to open his screen door to run inside, but I was right on his heels. Cornered, he turned around and held up his fists, so I backed down off the stairs. He seized the momentum and charged after me. I decided to keep at him, and wound up for another shot. But his fists were already flying. He pummeled me with punch after punch, and I was never able to land another hit. My mother's method clearly had its limits. I ran away, and he followed, but only pursued me to the edge of his yard, as I should have done. I ran home and nursed my wounds, basically a bunch of bruises and red spots. But I felt pretty good. Sure, there was a little pain, but it felt a lot better than living in fear of going outside. And I had gotten a good shot in on Chrissy, so he'd think twice about pushing me around again.

Once again, my mother had been wise and practical. And she taught me a lesson not by indulging my feelings, but by rejecting them. She essentially said, "Get over it." But that was just what I needed to hear. Like the win-win of tethering me when she needed to clean house, or letting me go free in order to teach me to avoid the street, my mother had the wisdom to know that kids needed to experience the hard and painful parts of life so that they could learn. And it also saved her a lot of time in the process. That's the practical part.

CHAPTER 3

BE SATISFIED

A
S A KID, I SPENT A LOT OF TIME LOOKING OUT OF
the window next to my bed. I don't think I have a
more vivid picture burned into my brain than the
view from that upstairs window. I love that picture. It means
home to me.

From my perch I could see all the houses across Lincoln
Street: the house that belonged to the Sullivans, the other Sullivans, the still more Sullivans, the Nichols, Mr. Cohane, and
then some more Sullivans for good measure. Bordering our
yard were the O'Briens, the Bugeaus, the Bucks, the Reicharts
and the Johnsons. My neighborhood was a place where everyone knew everyone else, and looked out for one another. Every
adult had a job to do and the kids were outside looking for
adventure. It is what small-town America is supposed to be.

When the weather was nice, I could sit at my window and

watch eleven different family tableaus of moms weeding flower beds, teens sunbathing, kids playing, and always men working on cars. People today rarely fix their own cars; back then everybody had used cars, and engine maintenance was a constant. Guys knew all the parts of the engine, and they weren't about to pay somebody to do the simple stuff like change their oil or replace a hose. If the sun was out, hoods were up, there was a beer on top of the air filter, and some father or older brother had themselves a nice greasy afternoon.

In our day-to-day life, parents may not have hovered, but authority was always around us, in the form of unseen adults. You could avoid them for the most part, as the out-of-doors world belonged almost solely to kids, but often without warning, a scolding from a phantom grown-up came from behind a nearby window. I would be engaged in some type of purposeless misbehavior—perhaps breaking a littered beer bottle and kicking the shards of glass down a sewer grate—and I would hear a voice come from a mysterious silhouette behind a screen door:

"Tommy Shillue! I know yaw fathuh!"

Who was that? I would think, as I ran away. *Probably LeBlanc again!*

"I know yaw fathuh, Tommy Shillue!"

Mr. LeBlanc had been upbraiding me for years, and I didn't even know what he looked like. It didn't matter if I was cutting through his yard, carving my initials in the tar on the street, or minding my own business, he always made it his business to let me know that he knew who my dad was. I guess it was supposed to scare me, and it worked—I'd always run. Fleeing from the scene of my crime was obviously pointless; Mr. Le-Blanc clearly knew who I was. Running away was a statement in its own right; it acknowledged that you had heard what the grown-up said but were not about to actually speak to them or do the unthinkable: apologize. The act of running away was both a guilty plea and a suspended sentence, leaving both parties satisfied that some justice was served.

Occasionally, however, we were thankful for the adults who kept watch on us from behind their blinds. One day I was in the crawl space under our front porch, which my dad used to store old lumber and other odds and ends. For me, it wasn't really a crawl space as I could stand up straight when inside. I was in there one afternoon, walking along the planks of wood like a man on a high wire when I came upon a big, thick nail sticking straight up from one of the boards, pointy side up. I put my foot on it and felt the nail push on the rubber bottom of my sneaker. The tip of the nail didn't go through, so I put a little pressure on it, surprised that the bottom of the sneaker still held. I put a little more weight on it, and carefully stepped up. I was on top of the nail, balancing right at the arch of my foot, the sole of my sneaker bending around it, but it still didn't pierce through. I remember the feeling of lightly balancing, nearly floating. In my memory it went on for a long time, but it probably lasted all of two seconds.

Then all of a sudden, I sank. The nail plunged through my sneaker and into my foot. As it happened, I thought to myself, *Of course that was going to happen,* which is probably the thought that follows so many of life's bad decisions.

The pain rushed in. I pulled my foot up with a good jerk and it slid right off the nail. I limped out into the sunlight. There was a little spot of blood on the bottom of my shoe. I started to limp through my backyard, trailing blood across the grass, and out of nowhere the ever-present Mrs. Bugeau came to my aid. A tiny, energetic mother of two, Mrs. Bugeau was also a mother to the whole neighborhood. When I was three, she had yanked me out of the Reicharts' aboveground pool by my collar when I was splashing helplessly after falling in.* She must have previously worked as a nurse or an insurance claims adjuster, because she seemed to have a sixth sense for medical emergencies.

"Don't move, I'm getting some bandages," she told me.

I don't know how Mrs. Bugeau knew I needed help because I don't remember screaming or crying, but perhaps I did. In my memory the entire scene plays out in complete silence, the only noise being the squeak of the nail going through my rubber sneaker.

When she returned, Mrs. Bugeau had me take off my sneaker and sock, and she soaked up the blood with a rag, then painted my wounds with Mercurochrome, a topical antiseptic that mothers everywhere loved to slather on anything that bled. It was a bright red color so just looked like more blood, making your wounds look more serious than they were, which was good, because every kid loves to have his injuries noticed.†

---

* Instead of the phrase "yanked me out," I should probably say "saved my life," but back then so many kids came so close to death so often, if you gave full credit to every adult intervention, the whole neighborhood would be lifesavers.

† The U.S. Food and Drug Administration in 1998 classified Mercurochrome as "not Generally Recognized as Safe" over fears of potential mercury poisoning. Well, I can tell you, if Mercurochrome caused mercury poisoning, me and all my friends would be Mad-Hatters because we almost never went a week without our moms painting an open wound with the stuff. Mercurochrome is a close cousin of thimerosal, the mercury-tinged preservative that was used in children's vaccines until it was accused of causing autism, which I also doubt, because I'm loaded with Hg and I feel just fine.

"This will stop infection," she assured me. "Those old nails are rusty!" She admonished me for playing in dark, hazardous spaces, and I let her think the whole thing was an unfortunate accident. Since I didn't understand why I had chosen to stand up on one foot and balance on the tip of a nail, I was sure she wouldn't, either.

The only time kids traveled on sidewalks when I was growing up was when they were with their parents. Sure, streets and sidewalks worked well enough, but we all understood that the best way to get from one place to another was through people's backyards. All adults told us not to do this, but of course, it was unthinkable to take the long way when there was a perfectly good shortcut through someone's yard. And, as far as childhood infractions go, this one was pretty minor so we pushed our luck. The path was often treacherous, with hazards that included hostile homeowners, lacerating brush, and angry dogs. We were suburban explorers and every yard had its own personality. Some had lush green lawns that were always wet, having been freshly watered twice a day. Others were even more groomed, surrounded with flower beds. These we avoided because we knew they were maintained by finicky owners. We went for messy yards with old cars up on cinder blocks and refrigerators lying on their sides with the doors removed, into which we'd climb and pretend we were in a space capsule.

One yard we visited frequently had a garden with all sorts of vegetables growing. I had no idea whose house it was. We'd crawl in on our hands and knees to avoid being seen, and locate the rhubarb plants. Then we'd pull a few up, pull the leaves off, give them a good wipe with our hand, and start munching. It was a deliciously sour taste, and my mouth waters just thinking about it. I know people usually take their raw rhubarb with sugar or honey, but I liked it right out of the ground. The taste went well with the stealth of the situation. Like most of our nefarious activities, we felt we were only forbidden *in theory* from eating whatever we wanted from someone's private garden. In practice, we were kids, and so like rabbits, we were yet another natural pest that a gardener had to deal with.

I remember Mr. Cohane, another fearsome old man, who passionately defended his property line, even though there was nothing there to protect—no flowers, no rhubarb, nothing. He looked like your average geezer, with white hair and horn-rimmed glasses, but he was not your run-of-the-mill "Get out of my yard!" type of old man, oh no. He was always in a tank top, with thick arms that had probably strangled Nazis to death on a beach somewhere. When he saw us cutting through his yard he would dart out on his back porch and shake his fist in the air. As we ran away, he'd always yell some detailed and creative threat, such as, "You see that barrel over there? Get a good look at it! I'm going to fill it with oil, light it on fire, and put you in it to die!" I'm not sure if he wrote those ahead of time or improvised them on the spot, but it always made us jump his fence as fast as we could into the Sullivans' yard. They did have a black lab named Casey, but unlike most dogs, he was friendly and well fed. This was not the case with all dogs in our neighborhood.

In those days, dogs had complete freedom to terrorize anyone who crossed their path, anytime or anywhere. There were no leash laws in Massachusetts, so if a dog caught you, he could do with you as he wished.

"Stay away from wandering packs of wild dogs if at all possible," my father once told me. And he said it as if it were common advice one would give to any child in the suburbs outside of Boston. But here is the reality: packs of wild dogs were quite common. I remember on several occasions rounding a corner and seeing a group of dogs running together in a surprisingly disciplined V-formation, like some dog version of *West Side Story*, looking for victims. I had seen them pull boys right off their bicycles and go to work on them, yanking their limbs in all directions. A boy's cries yielded nothing; no one was foolish enough to enter that fray. You could only look on from a distance and say to yourself, *I'm glad that's not me.* And chances are that when that poor kid returned home he would not be greeted with cries of "My God, my poor son has been attacked by dogs!" but rather with "For heaven's sake, look what you did to your clothes!" The prevailing belief was that if you could not avoid the dogs, you were somehow responsible for whatever they did to you.*

One Halloween I actually rang Mr. Cohane's doorbell. All the other kids thought I was crazy, but I was really just showing off and didn't think he'd open the door. He did, and to my surprise he actually had a smile on his face. "Well, hello, young man," he said. "And what are you dressed as this Halloween, a hobo?" Yes, I was dressed as a hobo. Also known as a vagrant, tramp, vagabond, or any other pejorative for "homeless person." Along with ghost, it was one of the most popular Halloween costumes in the 1970s, mostly because parents didn't buy cos-

---

* There was a dogcatcher in town, a laissez-faire public servant who would show up only in grave emergencies. He would use a pole with a neck-loop at the end to harness the wild cur and drag him into the canine wagon, never to be seen again. We didn't think much about the kind of cruelty and neglect the animal had suffered in its life. All we knew was, any dog that warranted a visit from the dogcatcher was beyond help.

tumes, they made them, and both of those costumes could be made from the rags and hand-me-downs bin in the basement.

"Why don't you step inside and see what we've got for you."

I did what he said (he was an adult) and stepped inside, then I turned to see my friends running along to the next house. They had written me off. He brought me into his dimly lit kitchen and told me to sit at the table. There didn't seem to be any Halloween candy anywhere. He went into his pantry and I heard shuffling. "Now let's see what kind of a treat we've got for you back here!"

I was thinking he must be putting the famed razor blade into an apple. But I didn't do anything, I just sat there waiting. He came out of the pantry holding a jug of apple cider, and poured some into a small Styrofoam cup. "Do you like cider?" he asked.

I took the cup, lifted up my mask, and started to drink.

"I love cider," he said. "Yes sir-ee, I've always loved cider."

As I drank I could see through the cider that there was something at the bottom of the cup, something round, and dark. Mr. Cohane had put something in the cider! He was poisoning me! But for some reason I kept drinking. When the cider was nearly gone I noticed there were three pennies at the bottom of the cup.

"THAT'S FOR YOU TO KEEP!" he bellowed.

I carefully sipped the rest of the cider and shook the wet pennies into my hand. "Thank you," I said, and he walked me to the front door. When I caught up to my friends I told them I got three pennies from Mr. Cohane, and they were jealous. What I didn't tell them was the plot of the horror movie that I had just experienced. I guess because I'd never seen one, it was hard for me to tell truly terrifying experiences from regular ones. I used to wake up in a cold sweat replaying that scene in Mr. Cohane's kitchen, even long after he had passed away.

Funny thing is, I'm pretty sure it was all a joke. As menacing as Mr. Cohane was, with the palpable flashes of anger and intricate death threats, I'm sure he was just a nice old man trying to have a little fun with the neighborhood kids, in his own weird way. But he had no idea how scary he was to us, and never once said, "I'm joking," so we took everything he said seriously. Oh well—too late now, I'm scarred for life!

Mr. Buck on the other hand, was the quiet, careful dad— a little too careful. One time his son Warren got a bunch of neighborhood boys together—me and my brother, along with John Sullivan, Kevin Sullivan, Joey Reichart, and Chrissy and Scott Sullivan (those last two were actually related) and built a sprawling fort in the Bucks' backyard. It had five rooms! We slept out in it for a week. It was, up to that point in my life, the most fun I'd ever had. Come to think of it, I'm not sure if I have to add the "up to that point."

The fort was situated deep in the bramble of their yard, far away from their house, and the first night we were sleeping out there, I heard footsteps in the middle of the night, and I could see the beam of a flashlight shining through the gaps in the plywood of the fort. It was Mr. Buck checking up on us, to make sure we were safe. *What a worrywart!* I thought to myself. *What does he think is going to happen to us . . . we're in a fort!* Truth be told, whatever danger we were in didn't come from the outside. There were so many rusty nails sticking down from the ceiling it should have been called "Fort Tetanus."

Our week of camping bliss came to an abrupt end when

Warren came to our yard and told us that his dad had disman-
tled the fort and taken all the wood to the dump. He claimed
that it was a "liability."

"What does that mean?" I said.

"He says he could be sued if someone got hurt."

"Sued? What does that mean?"

I honestly had never heard the word. It wasn't a litigious
time in America. I think the only person who sued anyone in
the 1970s was Ralph Nader.

Mr. Buck was just being careful. By today's hovering-parent
standards, he was doing the bare minimum. But for us, that
was too much. Cautious dads were no fun.

*

Still, there was a big difference between the bizarre, buckshot
terror of a Mr. Cohane and the more focused authoritarianism
of a Mr. Shillue. Kids still feared my dad's wrath more, because
men like him, family men, were more respected in the neighborhood.

A moment of great dramatic tension would occur every day
at about 5:30 p.m. That's when my father would pull in the
driveway and step out of his Dodge Dart in one of his business
suits. He had two: a brown one, which he paired with a yellow
shirt, and a gray one, which he wore with a blue shirt. I never
saw him in any other combination. Throughout his adult life
he stuck to this simple rule of men's haberdashery. He liked
hard rules and distrusted salespeople and magazines, so I'm
sure he came up with it himself, thinking, *It works, damn it.
Don't let The Bastards tell you otherwise.*

For as long as I can remember there have been *bastards* after my father. *Who were these bastards*, I wondered, *and where did they sleep? And why was it their life's mission to prevent this God-fearing father of five from pursuing happiness?*

I didn't know what The Bastards looked like, but over the years I've kept a running tally of all the things they are responsible for. Here are just a few:

- Preventing a man from making an honest living
- Writing textbooks that contained more "Socialist Studies than Social Studies"
- Taking us off the Gold Standard
- Creating the CD format just to make a man's entire LP collection obsolete ("Pretty soon they'll make those obsolete too. Mark my words, they're doing it as we speak.")
- Trying to get everyone hooked on Lipitor
- Canceling *Colombo, Gunsmoke,* and *Barney Miller* several seasons too early.

There was usually a group of boys playing in our yard when my dad got home, and when the Dart pulled into the driveway, all of them would immediately flee. They wouldn't even wait until he got out of the car. They would just bolt through the hedges, which drove my dad crazy.

"Damnit! Stay the hell out of my hedges!" he'd yell every single time.

Oddly, excessive concern for his hedges was the reason he was yelling, and yet his yelling was the reason the kids were always running away through the hedges . . . the very definition of a vicious circle. Neither party was really aware of the reasons for the other's behavior. My brother and I, the only two who understood, were not about to step in and mediate like a couple of diplomats—it wasn't our place. It was just too complicated to try to explain my dad to our friends. And there was really no compelling reason to do so. My dad never held us accountable for the behavior of the other kids.

That was the really good thing about my father, and something that other kids didn't understand. It was typical parental behavior to remain polite and civil in the presence of your kids' friends but to then let loose the fire and discipline when you got your children alone. That was not my dad's M.O. He had a very strong sense of right and wrong, but didn't care much for decorum or social niceties, so he was willing to blow his molten, ashy stack in the direction of anyone who crossed him, no matter whose son you were. But once blown, it would stay blown; he would never save it up for us after hours. We never bore the brunt, so to speak.

All of the neighborhood kids assumed that any guy who was that scary outside of the house must be a real nightmare behind closed doors, and so they thought my brother and I were an unfortunate pair. However, that was not the case. My dad was absolutely consistent and predictable. We knew the things that were liable to set him off, and thus we skillfully avoided the bulk of his wrath.

It was all about patterns. You just had to stay clear of him in the immediate period after he got home from work—as he checked the mail, got the domestic news report from my mother, and then went upstairs to change out of his suit and into his khaki pants and sneakers combo. After this nightly clothes-changing routine (picture the opening scene of *Mr. Roger's Neighborhood*, if Albert Finney were playing the title role) things eased up considerably. Then my mother got a little food into him, and he was as tranquil as a basking shark. His favorite dish was smoked shoulder.

"Ah! A shoulder! You're beautiful, Rosemary! Beautiful!" After wafting the smell from the pot, he would try to smother my mother with kisses as she shooed him away. The sight of my dad, this formidable man who struck fear into the hearts of all the neighborhood boys, begging for my mother's unreciprocated affection in front of the stove every night formed all of my ideas about love and marriage.

Then I would sit across the table and watch my dad contentedly gnawing on the shoulder like a bear, and picture the day I would do the same.

*

When I climbed into bed at night I had a routine. When everything was quiet except the crickets, I would sit up, crook myself into the window next to my bed, and look out over our yard. There were a few streetlights along Lincoln Street, but our backyard was completely dark. I'd look in the direction of the elm tree and wait, sometimes for what seemed like a very long time. Then, not always, but most nights, I would see it: the tiny orange glow would appear out of the darkness and grow brighter. It was the tip of my dad's cigar as he took a slow drag. When it reached its brightest, it would illuminate the bottom of his face and the underside of his brow for a second or two, and then die back down, and I'd sit and wait for the next glow.

I wondered why my dad liked to sit out there in the dark, under that elm tree all by himself. *Was it fun? Why would a man like to sit in the dark and not talk to anyone?*

Now I get it. I do the same thing. (Not the cigar, of course;

I'd like to, but with all the New York City regulations I'd have to walk too far from my apartment to actually enjoy it.) When I get home from work late at night, everyone is asleep, and I do the city version of my dad's ritual: I'll pour myself a drink and sit in the window of my apartment and look out at the dark cityscape. I'm the man of the house, and everything is quiet. There is something wonderful about the noise and chaos of a busy home, but to appreciate it you need some quiet time, some alone time. I may not have understood it, but I appreciated my dad's solitude, even back then. Now I know it was a way for him to savor his place in the world, his role as a father, as a husband, and as the mean dad in the neighborhood. He needed a chance to look out over his kingdom and be satisfied.

CHAPTER 4
BE THRIFTY

AS I'VE MENTIONED, MY MOTHER HAD A PHD IN TRITE aphorisms. One of them was "Find a penny, pick it up, and all the day you'll have good luck."

I took that to heart. I would keep my head down everywhere I walked, looking for my day's luck. If I found a dime, it was miraculous. Thrilled, I'd shout, "Ten days of luck!" I had an old-fashioned ceramic pig where I saved all my coins, but it had no opening on the bottom so the coins were essentially trapped. The idea was if you wanted to get at the loot, you had to smash the whole thing, so you'd be more likely to save up for something special. But my older sister Kathy showed me how to get the coins out by sticking a butter knife through the slot and shaking it upside down on the bed. How did older sisters know so many valuable tricks? Especially since Kathy had no older siblings to teach her?! It remains a mystery to me, to this day.

One hot day in the summer between kindergarten and first grade I took a butter knife and poked out what seemed like an obscene amount of money onto my bed. I filled my pockets with coins and decided I was going to go to Father Mac's pool, the local neighborhood hangout, and splurge on some treats courtesy of the ice cream man. I tried to be discreet as I walked downstairs past my mother, standing in the kitchen. I felt like a scarecrow stuffed with dimes and nickels instead of straw, and must have been walking bowlegged to prevent any jingling. This caused my mother to ask the obvious question: "Tommy, do you have money in your pockets?"

I didn't bother lying because my mother was clairvoyant and superhuman, and had the uncanny ability to call me on a lie *as I was telling it.* Of course, I probably had several obvious tells that could be read at ten paces by anyone over the age of fifteen, but my mother was the only adult I had attempted to lie to, so rather than consider that I might be a terrible liar, I credited her with mystical powers.

I emptied my pockets on the table, which revealed that I had seventy cents.

"Seventy cents! Where are you going with seventy cents?" she demanded.

"Father Mac's." I hadn't really counted the change. Even I was shocked at the amount I'd been carrying.

"Put that money back in your bank. Was it for the ice cream man? You don't need to spend money on him. I've got Popsicles." By "Popsicles," Mom meant that she had poured powdered drink mix into the ice cube trays and stuck toothpicks in them. My mother didn't need store-bought items when there was a perfectly good replacement at home. If she could make it herself, she would.

So when I suggested I supplement my piggy bank by selling lemonade, she indulged me. A penny saved was a penny earned, but an earned penny was even better than that.

I set up my stand with great care. The night before, I prepared the lemonade from a powdered mix that we had in the pantry. It was about a year old and dried out, so I had to crush the clumps of mix with a fork and stir vigorously once I added the water. I made several batches and put them in the fridge overnight. In the morning I filled our big orange plastic cooler jug—the kind that had a spout on the bottom. That way, I could easily serve my customers directly from the jug and didn't have to worry about pitchers and other messy things like that. We had plenty of Styrofoam cups; in fact, several sleeves had been in our back-hall cabinets for what seemed like years. As you may be gathering, Mom liked to hang on to things. You never knew when you might need them for things like, well, a lemonade stand.

We of course had an old schoolhouse desk in our basement, too, the wooden kind with the tops that open up, and it even had a hole for an inkwell in the right-hand corner. I dragged it out to the curb, put the jug on top, put the cups inside, and hung a sign on the front, written in my best block letters, ICE COLD LEMONADE. I set the price at a very reasonable two cents per cup. Even considering the value of a dollar in the early '70s that was an almost unheard-of beverage bargain.

"Where's the ice?" asked John Sullivan, circling around my stand on his bicycle.

"It's cold," I said. "I had it in the refrigerator overnight."

"But you've got to have ice—it says ICE COLD LEMON-ADE. Plus, the ice takes up space in the cup . . . you're going to be giving away too much lemonade if you don't have the ice in there. Don't you know that's how these businesses make money—it's almost all ice in the cups, so they're able to give you less of the drink."

I went in and got the ice—we had the old ice-cube trays with the handle that you had to crank back and forth to break up the cubes, while being careful that your other hand didn't get stuck to the metal tray. I put one tray of cubes into a trash bag and kept them beside my desk. Sully was right—one cube took up most of the space in the cup.

I did a brisk business. I thought I'd only get foot traffic and kids on their bikes, but to my surprise people would pull their cars over to the side of the road for a cup of lemonade. Most people didn't want any pennies back—they would give me a nickel, a dime, or even a quarter and tell me to "keep the change." I was refilling my jug all day and I went through all the ice cube trays in our freezer. By the end of the day I had between five and six dollars. I'd never in my life possessed such a large sum of money.

As I counted my day's receipts John Sullivan was strad-dling his banana seat beside me looking on. "What are you gonna do with the profits?"

"Huh?"

"You've got to reinvest the profits—that's what business is all about. You make money, you reinvest the profits in product for the next day's business."

"I was just gonna save it."

"You can't save it!" said Sully. "You've got a business now.

You've got to reinvest it. You should go to Dacey's and get more ingredients."

He was right—I had a good thing going and I should continue it. I felt like a real businessman all of a sudden. I got on my bike and John Sullivan and I raced to Dacey's variety store to reinvest the profits.

"Here, look . . . grape and cherry flavor Hi-C. You can offer a new type of drink to your customer."

I bought two jumbo packets of powdered drink mix for three dollars, and took my new product excitedly home to show my mother.

"What's that?" she said.

"I reinvested the profits."

"Why? That's a rip-off! Those cost a dollah-fifty apiece! I could get ten times as much for that price. And look—on the label, it's nonsweetened. You have to add your own sugar! I'm going to have to buy a big bag of sugar just to make this. It was a total waste! You wasted all your money!"

I shouldn't have been surprised. My mother valued thriftiness more than money itself. She would rather supply me with cheap, clumpy product than have me spend my own money on overpriced goods. I didn't blame John Sullivan for the terrible advice—in theory he was right about investing in my business, but I didn't live in theory; I lived in my house. I went to bed discouraged and never made another lemonade stand.

Kids are always being told they don't know the value of a dollar, but it's all a matter of perspective. Most adults think of the value of money in terms of things like real estate or educational expenses. But kids really appreciate a dollar's value because they think about small-ticket items. Back then, if I looked at a dollar, I'd see ten candy bars. And yes, you could get ten real candy bars for a dollar when I was eight years old.*

My mother was always teaching her children about value. But what if you get something for free? That's the best value of all, right? No, not-quite-two years earlier I had learned the lesson that there's no such thing as a free lunch (or snack). Especially if your goods have been *ill gotten.*

E.J. Shattuck Elementary School was an old-fashioned schoolhouse with one class per grade. Forget the 1950s, this place was closer to the Victorian Era. The school had a principal, but we never saw him; the real headmistress was the sixth-grade teacher Miss Gavin, who walked the hallways in a gown and pearls, and addressed the boys as "master" as in *"Master Shillue, stop that running and tuck in those shirttails posthaste!"*

The schoolyard was divided into boys' and girls' sides, for play before school and at recess. Both sides had equal real estate, but were used differently. The boys were spread out over every inch of their side—running, chasing, pushing, fighting. On the girls' side, they were clumped together like bees, around a thick iron bar. "The Bar" was about twenty-five feet long and ran parallel to the ground at the height of about three feet. Girls could play on The Bar anyway they liked, although it was too thick to get young hands around and too slick to sit or stand on. Girls would mostly hang on to it and chat.

I used to go to the border of the girls' side and watch them, clumped onto The Bar, buzzing. There I formed some as-

---

* Average price of a candy bar, U.S. 1970–1974: 10¢ for a 1.3-ounce bar; 1975–1979: 20¢, 1.2 ounce; 1980–1984: 30¢, 1.4 ounce; 1985–1989: 40¢, 1.5-ounce bar.

sumptions about the difference between the sexes: boys like to spread out while girls liked to cluster; boys like to fight and girls like to talk. Was this the natural order on display or a pre–Title Nine America shunting children into oppressive roles? I think it was a little of both.

The main hallway of school featured a massive antique oak bench. The Bench was where they sent the bad kids. A visit to The Bench for the day meant being watched, and judged, by all the other kids in the school. There was a flaw in The Bench as a disciplinary tool, however. Humiliation only works if one is humiliated. Because it was usually occupied by the older boys, and the tougher ones at that, most boys saw The Bench as a badge of honor. I was sent to The Bench only once, after engaging in a recess "snowball fight" using crushed beer cans (they were everywhere in the '70s) with two other boys, Johnny Heyn and John Mitiguy. My afternoon on The Bench with these two tough guys was a bonding experience, and we soon became best friends, with many more misadventures to follow. It seems The Bench, which was supposed to reform us through guilt and forced humiliation, was more of a door—to a world of hooliganism!

One day in my first-grade classroom at Shattuck Elementary School, Mitiguy turned around in his seat in front of me. (Most every boy in Norwood was referred to by his last name, maybe because so many of them were named John or Johnny.) With a devious smile on his face, Mitiguy held out a shiny coin. "Hey! I've got a quarter! I took it from my mother's purse. You want to go to Dacey's after school?"

A quarter could go a long way at Dacey Brothers variety store.

"You sure we can?" I asked, knowing what the answer

would be. Of course we could. I mean he had already commit-ted the crime of theft; now he had to get rid of the evidence. And he needed an accomplice.

So right after school we headed over to Dacey's, which was directly across the street. It was the afterschool hangout of many of the upperclassmen, the fifth- and sixth-grade paper-boys with money to burn. Mitiguy and I got their attention when we approached the corner store.

"Hey, kid . . . you want a sip of my Mountain Dew?" a deep (to me) voice said.

"No, thanks." I answered for both of us.

I knew what was up. There was a sixth grader who stood outside of Dacey's every day and offered any younger kids who walked by free sips of Mountain Dew, as long as they allowed him to pour a little on their head. I had fallen for his trick once myself.

"Just a little, you can take a sip, and then I'll put a tiny little sip on your head . . . you won't even feel it."

I knew it was a trap, but I didn't want to refuse because that could get me labeled a sissy and something worse could happen. I took the sip, and, of course, he dumped not one, but several sips of Mountain Dew on my head, which dried sticky, and stayed in my hair for the rest of the day. It was definitely not worth the sip.

So Mitiguy and I went in and headed straight for the penny candy. We could fill our pockets with sour balls, Mary Janes, and Squirrel Nut Caramels, and still had money to buy a Her-shey bar to split since they were only ten cents. Then we both bought a set of wax lips.

We stood outside Dacey's laughing and chewing. I tried to eat our haul fast because we'd spent some time in the store deciding what to get and I'd already be getting home later than usual. I didn't need my mother asking where I'd been. I finished up and probably didn't even thank John Mitiguy for treating me to that mound of candy, because kids don't really thank each other unless an adult is around.

I walked home at a brisk pace and told myself if my mother asked, I would say I walked home with Barbara Clarke, and that girls take a long time to walk home because they stop and look at things. When I walked in my mother immediately said, "Were you eating candy?"

I was completely unprepared for a yes-or-no question. I was sure it would be an open-ended, "What took you so long?" or "What did you do after school?" which would allow me to riff. But I couldn't riff on "Did you eat candy?" Not at all. I clearly had. I probably had chocolate smeared from my eyes to my chin from inhaling it so fast.

"Yes." I said, "Me and John Mitiguy got candy at Dacey's."

"Where did he get the money for that? He probably took it from his mother's pocketbook."

My mother was like Poirot and Nostradamus combined, and yet she never left our kitchen. Where was she getting her information? And why did I bother to fabricate excuses in advance, when she knew everything by the time I walked in the door?

"No more candy with John Mitiguy," she said.

The next day in school, Mitiguy turned around in his seat. He was grinning and holding two shiny quarters this time.

"Fifty cents!" he said, brimming with excitement.

"I don't know," I said. "I've got to go home."

"Are you kidding? Fifty cents!"

"Okay," I said.

We went over to Dacey's again and doubled our booty of goods: penny candy, the chocolate bars, plus bags of chips and baseball cards with gum. I hurried through eating it, said good-bye, and ran home. I don't know why Mitiguy liked spending time with me; I was obviously an ungracious dining compan-ion. When I got home I made sure to wipe my face and brush off any crumbs from my clothes before I opened the door.

The second I entered the kitchen my mother said, "Did you go to Dacey's with John Mitiguy again?"

It was ridiculous. I still don't know what gave me away.

"No more Dacey's with John Mitiguy! I know he is tak-ing that money from his mother without permission," she in-formed me.

The next day at school, Mitiguy turned around in his chair, slowly . . . holding . . .

"A dollar! I've got a dollar!"

It was inconceivable. I'd never seen a first grader with a dol-lar bill at school before.

"We're gonna buy so much stuff! This is it! One whole dol-lar's worth!"

I looked down to my desk. I decided I couldn't go through with it. I was fully intending to walk out the door of the school that day and run straight home. But all day John Mitiguy kept repeating "A dollar! A dollar!" and I never had the guts to tell him I wasn't going, so when school got out, he walked me over to Dacey's and I was an accomplice to a heist once again.

We got shopping bags full of stuff: Marathon Bars, Fun-yuns, potato sticks, and Lik-M-Aid. It was endless. We got onto the sidewalk and I started eating furiously, I wasn't even pay-ing attention to Mitiguy as he shouted, "Can you believe this? A dollar's worth!"

I looked up from my bag of Funyuns and saw the Volks-wagen bus coming down the street toward me. My mother and all her clairvoyance were behind the wheel. The gig was up. Without thinking I began to try to destroy the evidence. I threw the whole bag of Funyuns to the ground and started stomping on them. John Mitiguy stopped celebrating.

"What are you doing?" he asked incredulously.

I knocked the Marathon Bar out of his hand and onto the sidewalk, then stomped on it and twisted my foot, grinding it into the concrete. Mitiguy was aghast. He must have thought a demon had taken hold of me. I threw everything on the ground and started stomping on it, making a ground-up mix of choco-late and candy powder and chips and gum.

As Mitiguy screamed, "Why!!??" I saw the Volkswagen come upon us . . . and then drive right by Dacey's. I spotted my sisters in the back seat singing, and my mother was distracted by the cacophony inside her vehicle. She drove right by and didn't even see me.

I stood there on top of a mountain of snack-mush. John Mitiguy backed away from me, confused, and then turned and walked away toward his house, shaking his head in disbelief.

When I got home that afternoon, I kept waiting for my mother to confront me, but she never did. She really had missed the whole thing. I wondered how she could be so om-niscient and yet miss my heinous crime being flaunted right in front of her.

The next day I told Mitiguy that if he ever took money from his mother again, I'd turn us both in, although I don't think I needed to—he'd had enough of me when I stomped all over his candy like a boy possessed. I'd gotten off scot-free, but my actions haunted me for weeks. I would lie in bed at night and think long and hard about the value of a dollar and the price of all those snacks that I was so shamefully unable to resist, and even more shamefully wasted when I ground them into the street. For years I thought I had dodged justice that day because of my mother's uncharacteristic lack of awareness. But looking back, I realize it's more likely that there may have been a method to her negligence. She had stealthily put another one of her favorite aphorisms to work on me, teaching me a lesson more valuable than the biggest sack of candy.

A guilty conscience needs no accuser.

CHAPTER 5

BE COMPETITIVE

BEFORE CONSOLES AND GADGETS, THERE WERE just balls and bats; before gaming, there was just games. We played the backyard games that had been passed down for generations, and if we grew tired of those, we made up our own. And, there was a spirit of violence in our play. A game like Kill the Kid with the Ball was uncomplicated in description: you simply beat up whoever had the ball in his hands. Once he went down, the ball was taken from him and the next kid was ready to be "killed." Even the gentlest of games involved some type of jail that you had to escape or be freed from. Playground games have a survival-of-the-fittest ethos, where there were always winners and losers, and it became quickly known who was fittest, whether by skill or by ruthlessness.

We'd play the classic neighborhood games like Tag, Hide and Go Seek, and the greatest of all the tag games, Relievio. When deciding who was "it" in any given game, we'd stand in a circle and hold out our fists and recite the rhymes that every kid had absorbed through playground osmosis. Most of the rhymes involved some type of misfortune:

> *Engine engine number nine*
> *Going down Chicago line*
> *If the train goes off the track,*
> *Do you want your money back?*

Y-E-S or *N-O* spelled out on our fists determined who, through the process of elimination, would be "It." Sometimes it took most of the game time just to do the whittling down.

> *My mother and your mother were hanging out the clothes,*
> *My mother punched your mother right in the nose . . .*
> *What color was the . . . blood?*
> *Blue?*
> *B-L-U-E spells blue and you shall not be . . . it!*

It's amazing how these rhymes are passed from one generation of kids to another. I don't ever remember anyone teaching them to me; we all just seemed to know them.

All hiding games had a "ghouls," which had nothing to do with evil spirits. Maybe you had a "base," or "home base"; where I grew up, it was a ghouls. Ghouls was usually a tree or a stump, but it could also be a bulkhead or a picnic table. In our yard it was our big oak tree. In Hide and Go Seek, the ghouls was where you'd do the counting when everyone went out and hid, but it also acted as a safe zone. If someone who was being chased could get back to ghouls, touch it, and yell, "My ghouls 1-2-3!" they were safe for the time being. You couldn't tag them—you had to go out and seek others. Then when you were away, they were free to leave the ghouls and hide again. But you had to be careful about using ghouls too much. Someone who was always lurking near the ghouls was labeled a "ghouls-sticka!" which was just about the nastiest epithet any kid could be labeled. Kids were called names of all sorts, but in the caste system of suburban children, it was understood by all that there was nothing lower than a ghouls-sticker. There were no hard and fast rules about what constituted overreliance on ghouls; it was purely subjective. The idea was, you knew a ghouls-sticker when you saw one. That's what made it such an insult.

Buck Buck was a game of strength and stamina. There were two teams; one is the horse, and the other mounts the horse. The object is to collapse the horse. The first kid would be the pole, and then the next kid would bend over and grab his waist, and each kid would follow, grabbing on to the waist of the kid in front of him, making a long "horse." Once the horse was formed, the kid who was the pole would call out "Buck Buck number one!" and the other team would send their first player barreling toward the horse to launch themselves upon its back. You could use your hands on the backs of the first few kids to launch yourself as far as possible toward the pole. When the horse withstood the first mounting, they would call for "Buck Buck number two!" Kid after kid would jump onto the horse until it collapsed. As a member of the horse team it was crucial to crook your neck right up against the waist of the person in front of you and create a tight seal, lest someone land on your neck. And they would, too—that was the surest way to cause a cave-in because there are only two choices when a fly-ing kid lands on your neck, collapse or have your neck broken. While it was the horse team that was ostensibly the ones who were "in danger," it was almost always the mounting team that got injured. Pretty much every game of Buck Buck ended with a bloody nose after their face smashed against the back of the head of someone in the horse.

Red Rover was made for breaking wrists. Both teams would hold hands and make a chain, and take turns inviting someone from the other team to try to break through it. "Red Rover, Red Rover, send Jimmy right over!" and Jimmy would get running as fast as he could, aiming for what he thought would be the weakest link in the chain. If he broke through, he'd run back to his team. If they stopped him, he'd belong to them and take his place in their chain. The ostensible object of the game was to create the longest chain possible. But the real goal was to inflict some pain and suffering.

We'd battle against each other in all these violent matches until supper, when my mother would ring the cowbell and we'd come running. Then we'd barge in the kitchen and at-tack our supper. We took her big casseroles for granted; even though it was good and hearty, the stuff she prepared for us was surely not gourmet eating. Mom's food was sustenance, made for shoveling into the ever-burning furnaces of her growing children. Supper was not a solemn or sacred time in our house; it was a stop at a filling station. After speedily saying grace and making a hasty sign of the cross, we'd devour whatever was in front of us, put our dishes in the sink, and run out the door for the rest of our nighttime play. I used to see families on television, dressed well for dinner and holding hands to pray, with kids bowing their heads toward the napkins in their laps, and Dad at the head of the table. It seemed tedious and unnecessary. That was what we did on Sunday and Thanksgiving and Easter, but every day? My mother didn't have time to create some kind of Courier and Ives scene at the dining table; she was a stoker and we were the forge. She put dinner on the kitchen table and we ate it. And we wanted it that way—our daily routine was play, play, eat, play, sleep. We took it very seriously.

At night the games continued, and in the fall when it was dark right after supper, our go-to was Flashlight Tag. The rules for that game were simple—the one who was it only had to catch you in the beam of light to tag you. But if you could get a hand on him before he got the light on you, you had immunity for that round. The question was, should you try to hide out and not be seen, or go full ninja and try for the immunity. Flashlight Tag was my favorite game because it was the one game where it was most fun to be "it." It was spooky wandering through the pitch-black, but we all knew every inch of our neighborhood so well that it was still hard to hide from whomever had the flashlight. We'd keep playing up until the last moment when we were called in for bedtime.

There weren't just yard games, but a whole assortment of street and bike games, too.

One of our favorites was a bike game I'm pretty sure we made up ourselves called Numbers. One kid would ride out on his bike with a pad of paper, writing down house addresses. On a separate sheet, he would copy down just the house number without the street. He'd hand out the sheets of paper with a big list of numbers, *42, 528, 2132, 28A*, etc. There was no limit to where the leader would go to get the addresses; it was basically as far as he was willing to ride. Then the players would have to ride around trying to find the house numbers. As they found each number, they wrote down the street address after it as proof. Since many numbers repeated on different streets, all you needed was a valid address. (It didn't matter if the leader had written down *18 Maple St.*; if you found an 18 Winter St., you were good.) The winner was the first one to return with a completed sheet. Depending on the length of the list and the determination of the leader to collect addresses, this game could take all day. That was okay with us.

If we weren't making up games, we were playing the classics. City kids played Stickball, but suburban kids played the great American game of Wiffle Ball. Our yard was the unofficial Wiffle ball stadium, not only because of its ideal shape, but because a spontaneous edict by my father led us to rejigger the rules to create a quirky game. One day he came out of the basement after presumably hearing one too many Wiffle ball taps against the basement window and declared, "If the ball hits the house, it's an out!" Then he walked back into the basement and slammed the door. That became a permanent rule, whether my dad was home or not. But because our house stretched the entire left side of the field, it was hard to avoid. So, in an inspired bit of genius, my brother decided the drainpipe on the far corner of our house would be an automatic home run. Then, if a batter made good contact and pulled the ball to the left, it was either an automatic out or a home run.

It added the perfect bit of unpredictability to the game, and made for many upsets and come-from-behind victories. Whenever that rare ball dinged off the aluminum drainpipe, we all went crazy. Most kids would go all summer and just hit one or two drainpipe homers, but John Sullivan, the Babe Ruth of Wiffle Ball, usually hit one per game.

My brother's best buddy Sully lived right across the street. There were dozens of Sullivans around, but only one Sully. He was the kind of athletic kid that every other boy wanted to be. Sully was always the best at every sport he played, no matter what the season. He was tall and strong, but he wasn't just a jock. He had a physical grace that put him in a different category. In a foot race he would leave everyone else in the dust; when he played hockey he moved across the ice like a figure skater; and when we played Kill the Kid with the Ball we couldn't even get our hands on him. He would stop and spin like Fred Astaire then dart off in the other direction, leaving us lying in the grass wondering what had happened. He could also climb a tree without using his hands. He would get a running start and just dart up like it was a flight of stairs. Once time Mrs. O'Brien witnessed this feat from her porch. She crossed herself and uttered, "Glory be to The Father!"

I often think of Sully when I go to a Major League Baseball or NBA game. He still lives in Norwood and works as a mortgage broker, but it's impossible to overstate how much more physically gifted he was than everyone else around him growing up. If John Sullivan didn't possess the skill required to play at that level, it boggles the mind to think of the level of God-given talent in someone like Derek Jeter or Steph Curry. What was Jeter like in his hometown? He must have been all anyone ever talked about. With Sully, every Wiffle Ball game at our house was epic.

In our world if the sun was shining, there was always the noise of a game going on. Of course, we all got into trouble occasionally, but there were no thugs or hooligans in our neighborhood. For that you had to visit Marion Ave. It was a half-mile ride by bicycle if you took the roads, but by shortcut it was just two backyards away. For some reason it was just a little rougher over there. Marion Ave. was lined with big oak trees on both sides, which shrouded the whole street from the sun. Their thick roots burst through the sidewalks, and they would trip you as you walked. It almost seemed that the street itself was harassing you.

If you wandered onto Marion Ave., you were bound to have a run-in with Kenny Tebeau. Kenny ran that street, and like John Sullivan in ours, established the tone of the neighborhood. Kenny was physically strong, but sports were not his main interest. What he excelled at was intimidation, along with his silent, fearsome right-hand man Jimmy Bandanza. "Banna" always had his telltale red bandana tied snugly over his head like a skullcap. He had the whole package down—his name was Jimmy Bandanza, his nickname was Banna, and he always wore a bandana. For a twelve-year-old suburban thug he certainly had a very strong sense of branding.

The first time I rode onto Marion Ave. Kenny demanded, "Shillue! Hey, let me take a spin on your bike, Shillue!" If a kid asked to take a spin on your bike, especially an older kid, you had to say yes. If you refused, you would be, well, I don't really know, no one ever did. After the spin, Kenny handed the bike off to Banna, who promptly gave it a "ghost ride" and let it crash into a stone wall.

My only crime: being from a rival neighborhood. Welcome to Marion Ave., kid. In Norwood, the hierarchy of loyalty was neighborhood first, then pool, then school. So even though we all went to the same school, and all swam at Father Mac's pool together, if I decided to go over to a different neighborhood, I was on my own. It may have been only a few backyards away, but in attitude it was a whole different world.

For many years I avoided Marion Ave. But as my friendship with Heyn and Mitiguy grew, who were both from Marion Ave., I became interested in what was really going on over there. The influence of Kenny and his buddies was evident.

When we played street games over on Marion Ave. and teams were being selected, everyone was allowed to play, but they had to be judged first. They wanted to divvy up the teams evenly, so older kids would be more valuable than the younger ones. Older kids would be counted as two, younger kids would be counted as one, and little kids and handicapped kids would be considered half.

There was a kid named Michael, who had a leg brace and a weak arm and always played sports and games with the other kids. He bravely made up for his disabilities on the playing field: he could crook a hockey stick under his arm and get off a pretty good one-armed slap shot, and in baseball he caught and threw with the same arm. From the outfield, he could catch a fly ball with his glove, then quickly flip the glove up in the air; as the ball fell out, he'd snatch it out of the air with the same hand and throw it to the infield. It was pretty impressive.

But the way Michael was treated was not ideal. Calling him half a kid obviously was cruel, and it surely bothered him. But it had its upside. It made him resilient.

Did he want to be called half a player? No. He was not half a player and he knew it. And he proved it in every game. He wanted to play sports with us, so he was willing to deal with the requisite cruelty to do so, and he used it as a way to consistently exceed expectations. Michael was an extraordinary handicapped kid. Or as we called him, "one tough cripple."

There was also the kid on Marion Ave. who we called Himmy. His name was Timmy, but because of his very slight lisp, the *T* came out soft when he said his name, sounding a little bit like "Himmy," so that became his name. I never heard anyone actually tease him about it, even though you could say that his nickname itself was teasing, but it was used like any other nickname. "Himmy, you want to play hockey?" It never occurred to me that there was anything mean or inappropriate about his nickname until I was an adult. I'm not sure you could argue that there was any good that came of that, other than to introduce the idea to Timmy that kids will always be mean if given the chance. Perhaps Timmy was hurt by it, and early on made the decision to embrace it rather than being the victim. He never objected to his nickname. Maybe he just realized as a kid that he had to be tough to learn to deal with the world as it was.

From my street to Marion Ave., to every street in Norwood, these were the ways kids filled the hours after school back then. If we weren't sleeping, or eating, we were outside creating our rules, our hierarchy, and our fun. We didn't need adults to play with us or devices to entertain us. It may have been rough, even dangerous, and sometimes cruel—but it helped me learn a lot about human nature. The world is competitive. The world is territorial. You need to pick teams and have strategies and figure out how to win, but you have to follow the rules, too. And wouldn't life be more interesting if adults settled disagreements over a game of Buck Buck?

CHAPTER 6

BE CONFIDENT

I WAS LUCKY, I SUPPOSE, TO BE BLESSED WITH A HEAP-
ing dose of confidence as a kid. Plenty of kids struggle with
confidence, hanging in the shadows and staying quiet, not
wanting to draw attention to themselves lest they do or say
the wrong thing, or have their perceived faults pointed out to
them. Well, not me. I was a very confident kid—overconfident
even, but it wasn't because of any signals I was receiving from
the outside world. I was not very skilled in sports, but I always
wanted to play anyway. If I came in for criticism, I'd just shrug
it off. For instance, if I dropped an easy fly ball in right field,
my teammates might moan, but I'd simply pick up the ball
and toss it to the infield, yelling something like, "Just think if
I wasn't here at all! The ball would still be sitting right here on
the grass! Think about that! Look alive!"

I think my overconfidence stemmed from a combination

of things I absorbed in my childhood. As an adult, I've always been attracted to self-help books, life coaches, and anything that falls under the "motivational" heading, but I never really subscribed to any one doctrine or approach. I just skim the books in the aisle of the bookstore and think to myself, *Yeah that probably works.* But I almost always come away thinking, *I think I had that figured out when I was seven years old.* Just living your life back then was a self-help book. After all, most of what is taught in these books is pretty simple: they advise you to take a less emotional, more analytical approach to situations, so as not to let your bad feelings get in the way of doing what you want to do, and achieving what you want to achieve. I believe that I adopted that approach at home and on the streets of my neighborhood, through the constant exposure to a combination of strictness, moral clarity, independence, and pluck.

I love the idea of "pluck." I don't think it's something you're born with; it's something that's developed, and I think there was never a better laboratory to create pluck than the environment I grew up in, with its peculiar combination of 1950s rigidity and toughness and 1970s feel-good vibes. So I got a mix of lessons from my family and the culture of the day. My peers may have belittled me, but then TV's Mr. Rogers built me up and told me I was special. The behavior of the bullies at the playground was met with the solutions of my mother's time-tested aphorisms. My dad may have scared me into silence, and then Saturday-morning TV announced, "The Most Important Person in the whole wide world is YOU, and you hardly even know you!"*

---

* The Most Important Person was a series of animated short subject lessons for kids that appeared in between Saturday-morning cartoons. They were part of the "self-esteem" movement that was so prevalent at the time.

My parents' generation, all they got was the toughness. Kids of today just get the soft stuff. I was in the sweet spot.

I was overconfident, but not in an ego-driven way that had me walking around thinking *I'm great.* My calculation was more, *I may not be great but that's okay! Run the numbers and you'll see I'm pretty good!* This was aided by the fact that I was from the first generation to be raised on child-centric entertainment like *Sesame Street* and *Mister Rogers' Neighborhood.* Before these shows, the offerings were of the *Bozo the Clown* and *Captain Kangaroo* variety—basically strange-looking men talking down to kids and telling them to behave themselves and obey their parents. These new shows were developed by child psychologists and educators, and were very focused on building the child's self-esteem. We were constantly hearing messages like "You are special," and "There's no one quite like you." Most of our parents were still raising kids in the old-fashioned way, so kids of my generation were growing up in that small window of time where the people we watched on TV were much more loving and understanding than our own parents. Of course I loved *Mr. Rogers' Neighborhood*—he was more gentle and understanding than anyone in *my* neighborhood. I remember Fred Rogers singing:

> *It's you I like,*
> *It's not the things you wear . . .*

At age seven that line resonated with me because most of my clothes were unremarkable, and I'd been looking for a way to spin that into a positive trait. I always wanted nice, well-fitting clothes like those worn by Christopher Robin, the dapper boy from the Winnie-the-Pooh series. I knew I would have them someday, but for the present I had to wear mostly ill-fitting hand-me-downs.

Every year at back-to-school time, I wanted to do what the TV commercials told me I had a right and an obligation to do—to go to Bradlees and stock up on crisp new outfits for the fall. But my mother would always point to the fact that we had plenty of clothes that my brother Billy had just grown out of, "So those will have to do for now."

When I heard that Mister Rogers lyric I thought, *Yes, that makes sense . . . perhaps these clothes are not me, they are just hanging on top of me like a costume; underneath is a well-clothed boy like Christopher Robin.* I didn't wish to be a neat, tidy kid who never got dirty. Nor was I really into clothes or fashion. I was a regular boy who would ruin outfits the same day he put them on, but I was wearing hand-me-downs, so I felt like I deserved better. So what I was really asking myself was, *Why aren't my clothes living up to me?* A fair bit of self-absorption to be sure, but with the help of Mr. Rogers, I owned it.

I remember getting ready for second grade, and wanting to make a splash on the first day of school. Kindergarten and first grade had gone well enough, but I really wanted to get off on the right foot and make a strong impression in second grade. From my cobbled together hand-me-downs, I was able to assemble an outfit that looked like it was new. I already had a blue blazer for special occasions. I paired this with a nice white short-sleeve button-up shirt and a pair of knee-length dark-brown shorts. Then I added the kicker: white socks and black penny loafers, like the kid on the Buster Brown Shoes logo. I knew this combination was eclectic and different, as I had meant it to be. I wanted to push the envelope and get noticed on day one. I topped off the outfit with a pair of sunglasses (likely an old oversized pair of my mother's, plucked from the glove box of our car).

As I walked to school I knew my outfit was killing it. Passing drivers did double takes, and adults in their front yards smiled and said things like, "Well, hello there!" as I walked by.

When I got to school, I strode into class a few minutes late to get the full effect. It was immediate and stopped me in my tracks. The whole class erupted into laughter. Everyone. The guys. The girls. Even my buddies Johnny Heyn and John Mitiguy. In fact, they seemed to be taking a lead role.

"Ha, ha, ha! Nice look, Buster Brown!"

"Where'd you get those shorts, Bermuda?"

"Hey it's Joe Cool! Ha-ha-ha!"

I stared at them from behind my sunglasses. My face was flush, my head was warm, but it was a powerful feeling. My first thoughts, as I stood in that doorway, offer an insight into the way my mind worked: I had gone into school with the intention of having everyone look at me and think I was cool. Everyone *was* looking at me, but they thought I looked like a complete fool. And I, being so confident and with this amazing ability to shrug off criticism, remember thinking . . .

"Halfway there . . ."

You can't buy that kind of confidence. You can't learn it in a book or at a weekend motivational seminar. It goes deep. It's in the marrow.

Or, maybe, it's something missing—some tiny little part, like a hammer or an anvil, or one link in the DNA chain that most people have. Overconfident people are missing that little voice in their head that says, "Don't do that, it might not turn out well." They go ahead and do it anyway and work out the details later.

I call these preternaturally self-assured people dorks. I know that most people use names like *nerds, geeks,* and *dorks* interchangeably, as if they all describe the same type of person. They do not. Here's how it breaks down:

Nerds are aware of their social status and act accordingly. They become introverted, avoid sports, and, however reluctantly, gradually accept their lower social status.

Geeks are nerds with a specific skill set, such as writing computer code, from which their confidence stems. They didn't become confident until they started using their nerdy skills to earn a good living at a high-tech start-up, or as an in-demand freelancer with a massive hourly fee. Dorks don't need such recognition; the high self-esteem is built right in.

Dorks, just as I was, are just nerds with a lot of confidence. They refuse to assume their place in the social pecking order. Remember the nerdy guy in your high school who had no idea he was a nerd—he would walk right up to the popular kids at school and ask them, "What's going on this weekend?" and did they "want to hang, chief?" That was a dork.

I started out as a dork, but as I grew older, life slowly squeezed it out of me. I gradually became more conventional. The dork might have been gone, but the seed remained, and always will.

One example of my pluck that I am especially proud of is illustrated in a story I'd like to share from Father Mac's.* There were two pools in Norwood, Father Mac's and our rival, Hawes. We just called them "pools" but they were full-service

---

* The Father McAleer Playground. But no one called it that except my dad, who refuses to abbreviate. He sends packages "via Federal Express" and orders "Big MacDonald Sandwiches."

playgrounds and pools, courtesy of the local taxpayers, and the social hub of all summer activity in town. In pre-day camp and sleepaway camp America, this was how all the parents in town kept their kids busy until September. Theoretically both pools were open to everyone in town, but they were deeply segregated in practice. Based on your neighborhood, you were either a Hawes kid or one of the "FM Boys," and the turf war between the two was surprisingly potent.

"Fathuh Mac's Sucks!" I would hear from a passing gang of bicycle riders. It was remarkable how we developed such fierce loyalty to our local pools at such a young age. And it never ended—even in high school, when all the kids in town were in the same building, playing on the same sports teams and sitting at the same lunch tables together. Once summer arrived, all bets were off, and a Sunni/Shiite-like divide once again ran through the town, turning friend into foe.

At Father Mac's, some kids had money and some kids didn't, mostly based on age—the older kids had money from paper routes, yard work, or babysitting; some younger kids got money from their parents for the pool, but not me. If you did have any money, you had better keep it in the secret pocket of your bathing suit. Some kids left it in their sneakers while swimming, but that was a sure way to become the victim of petty theft—thugs and teenagers always looked in the younger kids' shoes first.* Every day when the ice cream man would arrive blaring his familiar tune, the kids with the money would go running, and the rest would look on with envy. I'd run, too,

---

* When I was a kid, the term "teenagers" roughly meant "juvenile delinquent" because when a bunch of them were together in a group, they were surely up to no good. It was only used in the context of a warning. "Don't go into that park—it's full of teenagers!"

but instead of joining the throng at the big window waving their wet bills in the air, I'd run around to the other side, pull myself up on the bumper, and yell through the driver's-side window at the back of the ice cream man's head, "Can I pick up trash?" I among a few of the other moneyless kids had learned how to make ourselves useful: the driver knew his truck was the source of most of the litter on the playground, so in the interest of being a good citizen and a champion of ecology, or, more likely, needing to remain in the good graces of the Norwood Department of Recreation to ensure his continued gold mine of a location, he would offer a free ice cream to diligent trash collectors.

We'd run around the playground picking up every scrap of litter. Despite a national shaming campaign against "litterbugs," most people in the 1970s were still content to toss their wrappers on the grass next to them. Some of the kids who were familiar with our routine would wait for us and dismissively throw their refuse at our feet as we came around. I welcomed it, though, because the more trash we brought back to the truck, the more likely the driver would be to continue our scheme. Once we delivered the trash, we could choose any of the first-tier treats as our reward—a Push-Up, an ice cream sandwich, a Fudgsicle, or a Nutty Buddy. It may be, to this day, the most satisfying job I've ever had.

If you were a kid with money and wanted to splurge, there was the flashy, oversized, red, white and blue Bomb Pop, which took advantage of our bicentennial pride. Walking around with the biggest, most patriotic refreshment on the playground was a way to bask in the greatness of Liberty. Think about what a testament this was to our preeminence as a nation: American children refreshed themselves by suck-ing on *huge frozen bombs.*

There was also the Good Humor Triumvirate, consisting of the Chocolate Éclair, Strawberry Shortcake, and Toasted Al-mond bars. These high-priced adult ice cream bars would sit untouched unless everything else in the truck was gone. They had too many layers of complexity to them, like a gourmet dessert-on-a-stick, and were not well suited for the playground. Kids didn't need that kind of subtlety while playing.

Father Mac's had its own culture. There was a list of fairly typical rules posted on the fence: no spitting, no cannonballs, etc. But there were also many unwritten rules. For instance, boys were not allowed to use towels to dry themselves. Towel-ing off was for girls. Guys had to drip dry. Any boy over six or seven years old who used a towel was a real sissy. I learned quickly not to even show up with one, lest it be soaked and used as a weapon against me.

As long as you didn't use a towel, you could dry off however you liked. One acceptable technique was to use the bathhouse wall. The dark-green paint absorbed the sun all day and got superhot, so the boys would line up with their backs to the wall, then flip themselves over like sausages and do the front. The wall stayed warm until the early evening, so late in the day when the air got cooler it would really come in handy. Some breezy nights late in the summer you could see a long line of boys with blue lips, shivering and fighting for wall space. They'd hug it tightly, and press their cheeks against it. Why this ritual was considered more manly than using a towel I'll never know.

When my friends and I were feeling adventurous, we would

ride our bikes to Hawes pool for a swim. Ostensibly it was to do something different and break up the normal routine, but we were obviously courting trouble. It was the excitement of going into enemy territory. When we arrived on the grounds it was like Wyatt Earp walking into Dodge City. The Hawes kids would stare at us. They thought we had a lot of gall to just show up at their pool and act as if nothing was amiss. They would mutter under their breath, but they couldn't do anything while the lifeguards were watching. So right after we were done swimming, we made sure to get right on our bikes and pedal out of there fast. Sometimes we'd discover that a few of the Hawes kids had left us a message, like a set of bent spokes to ride home on.

The Hawes pool kids were intimidating, but looking back, Father Mac's was probably the tougher pool. There were certainly a lot of young punks that hung at Father Mac's. At "the wall," a horseshoe-shaped structure with two high rectangular pillars at the entrance to the playground, brothers Billy and Dicky Barrett would hold court and improvise hazing rituals for the new arrivals. One that I remember (because I'd fallen prey) went this way: From the top of one of the pillars, Billy would drop a dollar onto the grass. Dicky would notice from the other pillar.

"Hey Billy, you dropped a dollar! Hey kid, pick up that dollar, would you? It's right there on the ground!"

When the unsuspecting kid bent down to pick up the dollar, Billy, who had been saving up a substantial lugie in his mouth, would spit on the back of his head. All the other kids would laugh, because they had all been victim to it in the past. And then Billy would stretch his hand down, and the kid would actually reach up and give the dollar back! You would think they'd walk away with it as payment for their humiliation, but that never happened. They knew they'd been beaten. Billy and Dicky were troublemakers, but they were nothing compared to the really bad kids at Father Mac's. I'd never seen them anywhere else in town, not church, not school; it was as if they existed only in the summer and only at the pool to terrorize the weak. They would hold court daily in the bathhouse, these huge hulking giants of teenage humanity who were able to grow a mustache at age ten. The inside of the boy's bathhouse was only about eighteen feet across—a long eighteen feet to travel. One rarely got through without some type of interference. They would sit wedged into the open stalls laughing and joking with each other, then pounce when you walked in, whipping you with a wet towel that had been twisted into a rattail. Man, those welts burned.

If I had to endure today, as an adult, anything close to what I experienced on a daily basis during those summers, I would be an unhappy man. Life would be simply intolerable. But constant harassment was just an accepted part of life as a kid. I wouldn't complain or ever think to mention it to any adult. "How was your day?" my mother would ask. "Pretty good," I'd answer, when in fact I'd just been waterboarded in the bathhouse showers by a gang of hairy teens.

One day when I showed up at the pool some of the toughs were in the bathhouse. Of course I didn't have a towel with me, not wanting to open myself up to ridicule, but I moved through as quickly as I could anyway. As I passed them one of them yelled "It's Tommy Shit-lue!" I kept my head down and exited into the pool area. I could hear their laughs echo from inside the bathhouse. "That's his name now! SHIT-LUE! Ha-ha-ha!"

I knew one thing—that Tommy Shitlue was not going to be my name. I didn't go in the water. I stood there in the sun-warmed puddle on the concrete deck and thought about what I should do next. I couldn't go squeal to a lifeguard, that would only make things worse. I wasn't about to go back in that dark, wet bathhouse and confront them. So, I reached down deep into my reserve of overconfidence, where I kept my pluck. Two girls walked by on their way into the girls' side of the bathhouse, and I decided to improvise. In an over-the-top carnival barker voice I bellowed, "Hello there! I'm Tommy Shit-lue!"

The girls looked confused and hurried away, but I could hear the tough guys quiet down on their side of the bathhouse wall. They were listening. Someone else walked by, and again I yelled, "My name is Tommy SHIT-LUE! At your service!"

Three more girls came out from the bathhouse on their way into the pool. "Hello there!" I hollered. "Tommy Shit-lue. Glad to meet you! Tommy Shit-lue, nice to see you! Tommy SHIT-LUE! That's my name!"

By now some kids were starting to gather to see what was going on. A lifeguard also came over to see what the commotion was all about, and I quietly told him it was nothing and decided to go for a swim. By then the tough guys had left the bathhouse by the other door. They had heard me using their name for me at the top of my lungs and thought they were somehow going to get in trouble for it. But I never said a word about them to the lifeguards.

And as for that nickname, I never heard it again. As I think back on my response, I realize I didn't come up with it all by myself; it was a little modification of my mother's "punch him back" technique. I didn't want to give them the satisfaction of upsetting me. And as she also used to say, "Nobody can make you feel bad without your permission." Call it pluck, call it overconfidence, call it being a dork, call it being quick on my feet—I'm just glad it worked. It wouldn't be the last time.

CHAPTER 7

BE CREATIVE

WHILE MY PARENTS WERE BOTH ON THE SAME page as far as faith and moral absolutes were concerned, they had vastly different styles. Where my dad was strict and intimidating, my mom was more artsy and slightly detached, probably because she spent her days at home caring for five kids. It would take a lot of energy to be as intimidating as my father all day long. He only had to muster it after hours, and on the weekends, so he could afford the energy to blow up when angry and present that generally scary figure that the other kids in the neighborhood ran away from when he appeared. Mom had to take a more 360-degree approach, lest she burn out too fast. Another reason she never hovered over us too much, beyond the fact that helicopter parenting hadn't been invented yet in the 1970s, was that she was always busy with her own projects. My mother's arts and crafts would become obsessions, and, like Picasso, her creative life was marked by distinct phases. There was her scrimshaw period, her painted-rock paperweight period, her calligraphy period, her industrial knitting machine period, and her soap-making period, to name a few.

Our house was decorated with my mother's oil paintings, scenes of nature—a pumpkin patch, a snowy cornfield, or a grove of birch trees. She went off to art class one evening a week with other Norwood housewives, women who today would probably be employed in the world of art, design, or fashion, but with big families to care for, had only enough time for art as a hobby.* My Mom did her best to make it more than that, and would display her work for sale at local art shows. Soon, though, she grew tired of oils and switched to another medium.

When I was very young she was still in her charcoal period, and we would all have to go to art shows while she did while-you-wait portraits, two dollars for black and white, or four dollars for color pastels. Her clients mostly consisted of parents forcing their kids to sit for a portrait, which was difficult for them, as you might imagine. She had to get the kid's happy expression down first, as it would inevitably change to an impatient scowl. We couldn't even sit still to watch them. The Shillues would all run off and play, then check in on the poor victim and my mother's progress later.

The portraits were very labor intensive, and she wasn't able to do that many in a day at a show—so being an entrepreneur

---

* If my mother were a career woman, she would have been as likely to be a mathematician or scientist. Her job before she married was listed as "computer." Like the women portrayed in films like *Hidden Figures*, she spent her days crunching numbers as a human computer.

at heart, she was always looking for a craft that she could mass-produce to drive up her profits. After a trip to the beach where my sisters had collected a bag of smooth rocks, my mother was so inspired that she confiscated the rocks and decorated them with paints and nail polish. She made them into little creatures like ladybugs and frogs, even buying googly eyes to glue on. Well, these delightful paperweights sold like hotcakes at the art shows! She even thought about going into the paperweight business and trying to mass-produce them, but again her artistic restlessness took over, and she switched to her next medium. A few years later, an enterprising ad agency executive name Gary Dahl created the pet rock, a plain rock with no decoration at all except for the googly eyes. He caused a national sensation and made a million dollars with what appeared to be a Junior Varsity version of my mother's paperweights. You can imagine our frustration as kids, but my mother shrugged it off.

Interspersed with her visual art were many crafts. The soap-making project was one of her most earnest, because she was able to combine two of her passions: craft-making and money-saving. In the spirit of Laura Ingalls, she began making her own bars of soap using lye and leftover cooking fat, pouring the mixture into tin molds. She strained the fat as best she could, but little bits of bacon and beef always remained. Although the bars didn't lather much, they did have a nice exfoliating quality. We complained that her bars smelled less like soap and more like whatever we had eaten the week before, but she persisted. She would change her formula slightly and make her soap bars more fun by using old make-your-own Popsicle molds that were shaped like cartoon characters, but that failed to make Mom's soap any more appealing. For that entire year, the whole family smelled like meat, but from my mother's perspective, she didn't purchase one bar of soap from the store, so it was worthwhile. My dad never complained, as he appreciated his wife's eagerness to stretch his paycheck and probably didn't mind smelling like smoked shoulder at the office, as it gave him something to look forward to when he got home.

After the meat soap it was back to art. Since her previous project involved materials from the seashore, she moved on to the next logical medium: scrimshaw. A great tradition among the seafaring men of old, scrimshaw is of course the art of drawing directly on the bones and teeth of whales. It combined art, history, and what I'm beginning to suspect was my mother's real passion: harvesting animal by-products.

We had a traditional dining room with a large dining table in it, but it was never used for meals. The room was always covered with my mother's projects, and the house was brimming with refuse and odds and ends. Was my dad happy with the house always in a state of artistic disarray? I don't know, but I never heard him utter a word of protest. And there was nothing he could do about it anyway, as he had married a woman with an artistic heart and no one was going to be able to keep her from her work.

Our home's rather "lived-in" feel wasn't only because of Mom's many projects. The ability to keep a tidy home slowly eroded with each child. *House Beautiful* was surrendered to *Kids Plentiful*. Only the moms who prioritized neatness above all other virtues could keep their homes tidy, and we all knew who they were. When I entered their homes, it was amazing—they looked like the sample rooms from a furniture store, or a complete showcase showdown, "New living room!!!" from *The Price*

Is Right. Their rugs were vacuumed in rows—you could see the diagonal parallel vacuum lines on the carpet.

One day I went to pick up something for my mother at Mrs. Bugeau's house, which was always beautifully turned out and ready to be photographed for *Ladies' Home Journal*. She left me in the foyer for a minute, and I wandered into the living room, which was so impeccably neat that I had to experience it up close. I was looking at the framed photos carefully displayed on the mantel when I heard a blood-curdling scream.

"Ahhhh! Noooo!!"

I turned to see Mrs. Bugeau in the hallway—she had almost dropped the mason jar she was holding. There was a look of abject horror on her face.

"Walk to the path!" she said quietly. "Walk slowly to the path!"

I had not only entered her living room, which was off-limits, perhaps to anyone but the gentleman caller from *The Glass Menagerie*, but I had also stepped off the clear rubber runners that ran through all the carpeted rooms in her house. My dirty boy's shoes were sinking into her immaculate carpet, and she was speaking to me as if I had stepped into quicksand.

"Walk . . . Tommy . . . walk slowly to the path!"

I walked to the runner, and then to Mrs. Bugeau. She reached out and hugged me to her like a released hostage, and quickly began to calm down.

"I'm so sorry, Tommy! I should have told you to stay in the foyer! I can't have any shoes on the carpet. God bless you, boy!"

I felt relieved that she was so relieved. Mrs. Bugeau had children—her daughters were friends with my sisters—and I wondered what it would be like to grow up in that home. I appreciated its beauty, but to me it didn't seem like a home—it was so delicate. It didn't feel comfortable. I preferred our disheveled den.

After the brief scrimshaw period my mother moved on to knitting. She had actually always knit and taught us all to knit as well, the boys as well as the girls. I remember sitting around the television, all of us watching *Ben-Hur* as we stitched away. I never really had any projects of my own, but my mother would give me her projects along with instructions, and I'd do the easy rows in the middle. To this day, my sister knits almost everywhere she goes. Sometimes, I'll be waiting to go on at a comedy club and one of the comics will come off shaking his head, saying, "Weird crowd. There's a woman right up front knitting."

"Oh, yeah," I'll say, "that's my sister."

One day, for some reason, my mother decided to kick the knitting up a notch. When a huge package arrived via parcel post, she eagerly unboxed her latest project to take over the dining room—a massive industrial knitting machine. With it, she declared, she could complete projects hundreds of times faster and sell many more items, even though moving my mom's projects to market was usually more of a demand than a supply problem. In the world of today, with Etsy and eBay, she may have been able to find customers by the thousands, but back then she had to be content with whoever wandered by her tiny booth at the craft fair. Nevertheless, for the next year, every night of the week we heard the constant crunch of the knitting carriage running back and forth across the hundreds of hooks and needles, creating sweaters, scarves, hats and mittens, and even Nativity scenes. Yes—knitted versions of Jesus, Mary, Joseph, and the Wise Men along with little knitted donkeys and sheep. Some of the items would be sold at craft fairs, but most would be given as gifts. At birthday parties and housewarmings, any one of the Shillues could be counted on to show up with a knitted gift, and sewn into each, the label "crafted by Rosemary Shillue."

At some point, probably around my mother's normal eighteen-month window of exhaustion, she took the knitting machine up to the attic, and we never saw it again. Its place on the dining table was then taken by a machine of approximately the same size and shape: an industrial yogurt maker. My mother had read that the active cultures in yogurt could make Westerners live as long and healthy as Tibetan monks, who could walk up a mountain without breaking a sweat. We all must eat yogurt, she decided, but it was much too expensive to buy. So, she would make her own. Overnight the dining room became a pasteurization lab. Maintaining the correct temperature of the milk products became very important, so we were not allowed to walk through her delicate thermophilic environment during peak manufacturing. Once again, the emphasis was on production, not need, so even after gifting yogurt to everyone in the neighborhood, there was plenty of product left, which we of course had to eat. Little Miss Muffet herself would not have been able to put away the volume of curds we were consuming on a weekly basis.

Her projects never ended. To this day she has an attic full of watercolors of the famous swan boats on the Boston Public Garden, which she has mounted on framed mirrors. She calls them "Boston Mirrors" and she thinks they would look just perfect in your home (and is looking for a gift shop interested in selling them—she still has a little trouble with Etsy). So far I've given about ten of them as gifts. But here's the thing about my mom and all of her projects: they sprung from the same qualities that she put into everything she did, things that rubbed off on me. A relentless creativity, combined with a desire to produce goods that serve a purpose, and also make some money in the process. She loved art, but her attitude was, "Why work so hard on something if you don't make some money?" Even though her projects were never a "success," she just moved on to the next one, and never considered any of them a failure. As of course, she shouldn't have. She had had to put her creativity on the back burner in order to raise a family, but she always kept it simmering, always kept busy, kept working and creating. I like to think I'm the same way, so you can go ahead and hang the tag on me: "crafted by Rosemary Shillue."

CHAPTER 8

BE DEDICATED

SO MANY OF MY BEST CHILDHOOD MEMORIES IN-volve baseball. I used to love listening to the Red Sox games with my brother on our transistor radio. Not all the games were televised back then and there weren't any cable packages, so listening to the radio was the main way that fans experienced the games. You'd hear each play described in detail by the play-by-play announcer, with the faint sounds of the stadium in the background, and your imagination had to do the rest of the work to bring the baseball diamond alive. I had forgotten how good listening to baseball on the radio was until my wife and I moved into an old loft down by the East River in the DUMBO area in Brooklyn. The Red Sox were playing the Yankees for the pennant (which everyone calls the ALCS these days, but I like "the pennant!"). We moved into our apartment halfway through the month, on October 15, and the power and cable had not been turned on yet, so I went up on our roof and listened to the Yankees play the Red Sox in game 6 of the pennant on my transistor radio.

I was looking at the Brooklyn Bridge stretched out before me, a fog rising up from the East River with the Manhattan skyline behind, listening to the announcer deliver the play by play as the Red Sox came from behind to win 9 to 6 over the Yankees. It was probably the best baseball game I have ever listened to, followed the next evening by the most disastrous. The Yankees won game 7 in extra innings.

That was in 2003, and it was the perfect setup for 2004, when the Sox swept the Yankees for the pennant and went on to sweep the Cardinals for the World Series, their first in nearly a century. It all happened so fast, no one knew how to react. My wife and I were in a new apartment by then, living downtown in the Financial District of Manhattan, and after I watched the Sox win it all from the coziness of my home I forced my wife to go out to celebrate with me. (These are the kinds of things you can do before you have kids. I'm sure Denise misses our late-night coerced celebrations as much as I do.) We crossed the street to Jim Brady's Saloon, which had already closed its doors, because everything shuts down early in the Financial District. I had to bang on the windows and beg the bartender to open up. I demanded to be let in to celebrate the Red Sox historic World Series win. He didn't even know it had happened; he was watching reruns of *Will & Grace*, as he did every night. My wife and I sat at the bar and drank Guinness while he cleaned up.

*

The first Red Sox game I attended at Fenway Park was in 1973 when I was seven. The Father Mac's playground had a school bus in the parking lot to take us to the game, and my mother sent me along on the bus with the playground "chaperones," who were really just young teens who also hung around the playground. My daughter is seven years old now, and I can't imagine sending her off to Yankee Stadium by herself, but such was the way of the world back then.

The Sox were playing the Texas Rangers, and our tickets were out in the right-field bleachers. I couldn't believe how close we were to the pitchers warming up in the bullpen. I also couldn't believe how big and beautiful and packed with people the park was. The biggest thing I'd ever been in up to that point was a one-ring circus tent.

The first pitch was thrown at 2:12 p.m. in the afternoon. The great thing about baseball's obsession with statistics is that every moment of every game is recorded for history. I can look at the box scores of that afternoon game from 1973 and relive every inning. Looking over a bunch of numbers in rows and columns, it all comes rushing back to me. Bill Lee "The Spaceman" was pitching for the Red Sox. Dwight "Dewey" Evans was playing right field, Carl "Yaz" Yastrzemski was in left. Great team, great nicknames.

I cheered along with the other Father Mac's kids and the rest of the bleacher creatures. I heard some salty language. I ate some salty popcorn that came in one of those paper cones that you could use as a megaphone when you were finished. The Red Sox won 6 to 5, making it a perfect ending to my first live game. When it was over we all got up and started the slow march out of the stadium. The moving mass of people was daunting—I was so small that I was looking at people's belts. My mind wandered as I walked; I read the big sign that said SECTION 10-C, I watched the men closing up their concession stands. And all of a sudden I noticed that I wasn't around anyone I knew. I stepped to the side and let some people by. I looked for a familiar face in the crowd where there was none. I slipped back into the turgid whirlpool of people and continued in their direction. Eventually someone put his hand on my shoulder.

"You lost, kid?" he said.

He surprised me because I was trying very hard to look unlost but I think my height gave it away. I said, "Yeah."

"Follow me, I'll get a cop."

In just a few steps, he flagged an officer who took me aside. We were at the gates, and people were flowing through the turnstiles. He asked me my name and I told him; he asked who I was with and I said, "Father Mac's." I guess that was all he needed.

He picked me up and sat me on one of the turnstiles, with my legs dangling off the back. I watched person after person go by as they exited the park. I guess the idea was, if my people were still in the park, they'd have to see me on the way out. After a while I saw a different cop approach with a little girl in his hands. He plopped her on top of the turnstile next to me. It was Kathy Barrett, from Father Mac's. She was alone, too. She'd come to the game without her brothers Billy and Dicky, and I'm pretty sure we had both been thrilled to be there without our older siblings, but now we were both lost. She looked over at me and smiled. We couldn't really talk because there were people streaming between us, but I was glad to have a companion during my stint as an orphan. After about an hour, which was probably really only five minutes, a Father Mac's playground chaperone grabbed my shoulder. "Come on, you two!" he said, clearly irritated. He ran us up the street and around the corner to an idling line of yellow school busses. We went to the back, found a seat, and rode home together, and we bonded over our shared experience. I don't know if Kathy Barrett remembers that bus ride, but I've always considered that my first date.

*

Baseball is always portrayed as a father-son experience. Ray from *Field of Dreams* fantasizes saying to his father, "Hey, Dad, you want to have a catch?"

That wasn't my experience. Mine was more like Harry Chapin's "Cat's in the Cradle" without all the sadness. Little League was one of those things your parents signed you up for to get you out of the house and off their ledger for an entire season. That's the way kids and parents wanted it. Except for the kids whose parents were coaches, moms and dads did not spend much time at the ball field. It wasn't like today, where parents are fully kitted out for weekends of kids' sports competitions, chairs, coolers, and enormous cameras ready to record every second. Little League baseball was about six innings away from that scowling authoritarian you lived with, in favor of the scowling authoritarian you barely knew. It was a gift to parents and kids alike. I didn't want my dad at the game. I already had a grumpy adult critiquing my performance.

One of my Little League coaches was a middle-aged man who appeared to have no kids, or no family whatsoever. He would show up for practices and games with only his tobacco kit, sit on the end of the bench and pack his pipe for the first three innings, and the rest of the game smoke it. He said almost nothing, just occasional orders yelled out between puffs. If we were downwind of him, we'd all be enveloped in a cloud of smoke, but I loved it. To this day the odor of pipe tobacco means baseball to me.

I wasn't terrible at sports. I just wasn't great. I had a certain amount of physical coordination and speed, but I never had a lot of strength, so at team sports I was always a fair-to-middling presence. I also lacked the killer instinct, so instead of the "thrill of competition and absolute will to win," I played more from the "deep desire to not end up embarrassing myself."

The greatest indignity was being called out on strikes while at bat. Letting a ball pass by and hearing "strike three!" was the most sinking feeling. There's a reason that "go down swinging" is an expression and a positive one. But for most kids, it's much too tempting to try to hold out for the possibility of taking a base on balls—it's the chief way that Little Leaguers reach first base. There were only two or three players from any team who consistently made contact with the ball; most kids would pass their time in the batter's box hoping the pitcher would miss the strike zone.

Thus, each at-bat was a charade, and I had to establish credibility. By taking a healthy swing at the first pitch, I was establishing an aggressive posture so no one could ever accuse me of passively courting a walk. Swinging first ensured I would never "go down looking" as there was nothing worse than letting three strikes go by without a swing.

When I let a strike go by I'd turn and see a smoky cloud yelling "Keep your mind in the game!" "Stay focused!"

The thing is that I was very focused—my mind was in the game, it's just that my body wasn't.

Here comes the pitch . . . my mind would tell me. *It's definitely coming over the plate, but it's a fast one, and if I'm going to swing, I probably should have started by now . . . guess not.*

"Strike two!"

Baseball is actually a cruel sport for kids for this reason: Little Leaguers are the same age only in theory. The skill differences at that age are so pronounced as it is, but when one kid is eleven months older than another, it creates an unfair advantage comparable to steroids in pro sports. If I'm a kid born after Thanksgiving and you're a kid born in January, you're basically juiced.

Luckily, as a result of my aggressive desire not to look like an idiot, I was not seen as one of the pathetic players. I wasn't pulling my team to any victories, but I wasn't dragging them down either. I spent a lot of time on the bench shooting the breeze with the rest of the mediocre players. (The good ones tended to stick together, as did The Pathetics.)

I remember my one big game like it was yesterday. I was on the bench with Steven Power, and as usual I was having an unremarkable afternoon. We were down by 2 runs late in the game. And, for reasons still unknown to me I began to engage in some fearless braggadocio.

"When I get up there I'm gonna do major damage to that ball. Major damage."

"Major damage?" asked Steven.

"Major league damage. First of all, I'm going to hit a home run. Over the fence—the center-field fence. I'm going to hit a line drive right over the center . . . a frozen rope to center. It'll be over the fence before the pitcher turns around to look at it."

"There we go!" said Steven. I wasn't done, though. Oh no. Not at all.

"The ball is going to be so far in the woods, they won't be

able to find it. And when I run the bases, I'm going to take these cleats"—I said, pointing to my new metal cleats—"I'm going to take these cleats and put holes in all the bases as I run around them."

"Yeah?"

"Yeah," I said, standing up and demonstrating. "One, two, three, four, five, six"—I pointed to the six cleats that lined the front bottom of my shoe—"I'm gonna make six holes in every base." I demonstrated to Steven Power how I was going to round the bases, stabbing my cleats into each base and turning my foot, grinding and ripping the base open. I don't know where the idea came from, but I was swept up in the excitement of my brag.

"Can you do that?" asked Steven.

"I will do it," I said. "They're gonna need new bases."

Then came that booming voice: "SHILLUE! Get a helmet on! You're on deck!"

I hadn't even been paying attention to the order. I was so focused on building my fantasy athletic triumph for Steven Power.

I took my resolve with me to the plate. I now had to show Steven Power that I wasn't completely full of it. I stepped up to bat. I saw that we had runners on first and second base. As I slipped into the batter's box, I had a steely expression like Clint Eastwood, but I was relaxed. The first pitch came quickly. It was a fastball straight over the plate. I took a nice, easy, confident swing . . . and connected directly in the center of the bat. It was the most effortless I'd ever swung, and the most perfect connection I ever made to a ball. It just clicked off the center of the wooden bat—not a big crack, just a knock, like a single knuckle on a pine door.

And as I ran to first base I saw it sail over the head of the center fielder and over the fence, just as I said it would. The ball was in the woods before the pitcher even turned around. I could see the first base coach jumping up and down in shock. I could hear my team thundering from the bench. I had just hit a game-winning home run! My team was crowded around home plate screaming, and I could see Steven Power standing there with his mouth agape. Then I remembered my promise to Steven; I hadn't been puncturing the bases! I'm nothing if not a man of my word, so despite being a few steps past second . . . I ran back to it and jumped on the base. Nothing happened. I stomped harder. I got both feet on the heavy canvas bag and jumped as hard as I could, trying to keep my toes stiff so the cleats would stab through the fabric. Nothing. Three more times I jumped, ferociously trying to break through.

"What in hell are you doing!" the third base coach yelled at me. I looked up and both teams looked on in shock. *Was this kid losing his mind? Did he not know what a home run was? Did he have some score to settle with the second base bag?*

"RUN!" they were all yelling. I started up my run again, and as I rounded third, I took another stab at leaving some holes in it, but it was no use. As I headed home, my puzzling behavior at second base was forgotten. The home run was enough of a surprise to negate my crazy base jumping. My cleats hit the hard surface of home plate and I bounced up, but didn't come down . . . I was already up in the air, being pushed up by twenty or so hands that carried me back to the dugout.

My love of baseball continues to this day. It is the most American of pastimes, and although very few people can master it, almost anyone can do it and have a good time. For a mediocre player, you can find joy in being part of a team, but the fleeting moments of individual glory, those you can savor forever. When I replay that game-winning home run in my mind, I can see the baseball diamond laid out before me and hear the faint sounds of the game as if they are coming through an old transistor radio. When the coach dropped me off after the game that night, I jumped out of the back of his pickup and walked into my house as my teammates chanted "HOME RUN KING! HOME RUN KING!" I thought to myself *I've got to remember what this feels like.* I knew that would probably be my one and only Little League home run, and as it turned out, it was. But one is better than none. I'll take it. I don't even remember all those pop flies I missed.

CHAPTER 9

BE RECKLESS

I COULD ALWAYS SENSE IT THE SECOND I WOKE UP. SNOW cover created an unmistakable sound blanket; the world outside was noiseless. I'd flip up my window shade and get blinded by the white and think . . . *snow day! Snow day?* We still had to check the radio. We'd huddle down together to wait for our town to be read out. Andover, Attleboro, Ayer . . . All Schools. Bainbridge, Braintree, Brighton, Burlington . . . All Schools. We had to wait all the way to the *N*'s to hear "All schools . . . Norwood!"

Winter lasted forever in Massachusetts when I was a kid. I don't know if the U.S. weather service or the *Farmer's Almanac* will back me up on the facts, but I'm going to trust my memory on this. Sometime around Thanksgiving the snow would begin, and the world would turn white. Snowstorm after snowstorm would pile one on top of the other. Our backyard would be covered under at least two feet of snow at any given time. The three-foot hedges that lined our yard became just a little speed bump around the edge of our property; we wouldn't see them until the Ides of March. All the sidewalks in our town disappeared, buried by the runoff from the snowplows. Sidewalks became snowbanks. You had to walk in the streets—a dangerous proposition because they were a narrow maze covered with a thin superpacked, ultraslick layer of snow and ice. If you didn't have chains on your tires, good luck. As I was out walking I'd frequently see a car crawling down the street toward me trying to gain traction, its rear end sliding back and forth like an overweight water-skier, banging into the snowbanks on each side. I'd crawl up on the side of the bank and let it go by.

Driveways were just trenches—most people just dug out a car-wide path so they could get to work. Occasionally you'd see someone who did their civic duty and shoveled out the whole sidewalk in front of their home, but what good did it do? The clean sidewalk ended abruptly at their property line, and you had to either climb back up the snowbank or walk back out in the street.

My dad didn't make us shovel the sidewalks, but he did insist on us shoveling the whole driveway to the edge of the concrete. We considered him a real tyrant on this issue, but he knew if he didn't enforce this, with each successive snowstorm his driveway would get smaller, and by New Year's he'd be squeezing into a car-sized wedge and not be able to open his car door.

The magic of a snow day was quickly smothered by the reality of our shoveling duties. We'd just finished jumping up and down after hearing the "Norwood . . . All Schools" message on the radio when my dad would walk into the kitchen with an expression that said, *Oh yeah? What's so good about it? Put on your boots and grab a shovel.*

Shovel is actually an aspirational term for the tools we had to use. *Spade* is more accurate. My dad never went out and bought actual snow shovels—you know, those glorious, wide-mouthed beauties made of lightweight aluminum, with ergonomic handles, designed so that you can actually lift them over your head without strain. No, Dad was content with his three garden shovels, with the thick wooden handles and rusty iron mouths, difficult to lift even *without* any snow on them. These were more suited for digging a cemetery plot than clearing snow. Two of the three were actually spade-shaped at the front; they came to a point! Each scoop exposed only a thin line of driveway in front of you. Sisyphus himself would be looking down on these two boys and laughing. Regarding most housework, my dad was egalitarian, and the boys and girls all had to work, but when it came to shoveling, raking leaves, and mowing the lawn, these three were boys only. My sisters, although avid proponents of women's liberation, never complained.

Like the Don't-Mention-McDonald's rule, my brother and I wished in silence for our dad to someday buy some real snow shovels, but we never asked him to. The truth is he probably would have bought them for us—anything to increase our work output, which was, I'm sure from his perspective, unimpressive. I'm now judging from my own kids, but anything I ask them to do, whether it's "Clean up your room" or "Put on your shoes," leaves me thinking, *How is it possible that this is taking them so long?* But unlike my brother and me, my daughters have no problem asking for assistance or letting me know exactly how they feel about the task I've assigned them. This is another area where I could use a little more internal Darth Vader; it would make my life a lot easier. Chalk up another one for my dad's parenting style. Mean dads for a better America, I'm telling you.

After we finally finished with the driveway, we hit the slopes. There were a couple of really good sledding hills in town. St. Catherine's church was one, where there was a massive hill in the back that led down into the parking lot. On the first morning of a snowstorm, the hill was just about perfect.

Of course, sledding technology was not what it is today. Most of us had the old Flexible Flyer–type sleds with the metal runners on them, oddly named because these were the least flexible pieces of equipment imaginable. These sleds worked well, but only in certain conditions. The snow had to be hard; if too powdery, the blades would scrape through to the ground. If the snow was too deep, the blades would sink in and the wooden base would just hit the snow and drag to a stop. But with solid-packed snow, or on ice, those things would fly!

We didn't have the best sleds, but at least we had them. There was always one kid who showed up with a trash can lid that his mother gave him to use. "This is what I used to use! It worked fine!" I'm sure she told him, but of course they never did. We pitied the lid kid. We also knew how he felt, since our mother subjected us to many of her own winter hacks. She made us wear Wonder Bread bags on our feet. The kids called me Wonder Boy. Now, I remember wearing these bread bags as *my actual boots*. My mother swears that she used these as boot *liners*, which helped the boot slide on easier, and helped keep socks dry. I'm sure she's right, but I must have lost my boots during a run one day and just kept on sledding, because I distinctly remember the experience of trudging up those hills in nothing but the Wonder Bread bags.

*

Back then there was zero talk of climate change. There did seem to be a lot of concern about a hole in the ozone layer, but we weren't really clear on what the ozone layer was, and apparently all that we needed to do to keep the hole from getting any bigger was for adults to switch their hair spray and deodorant from aerosol to pump bottles. The only thing we kids knew about the weather was that snowstorms were a gift from Almighty God, who obviously created them just for us. He wanted us to wander the drifts to do whatever we pleased—sledding, ice caves, igloos, which we did until it became very dark or we got so hungry we had to go home and demand food from our mother.

Then it arrived: 1978, and with it, the Blizzard of '78. News of the coming Blizzard had been circulating for, it seemed, months. Michael Dukakis was the governor at the time, and everyone in Massachusetts watched him on TV with his Irish cable-knit sweater and a shovel in his hand, his wife Kitty by his side, telling everyone to remain calm. It was such perfect political imagery—shoveling snow with an Irish sweater with his Greek head sticking out of it, as that was about as multicultural as it got in Massachusetts. It was that winter that people started talking about Michael Dukakis as someone who could be President someday. And you know how that worked out.

Every snowstorm my brother and I prepared for the dreaded shovel duty, but miraculously, the Blizzard of '78 was so overwhelming, that we were off the hook—the whole state was to be hopelessly buried for at least a few days. So as the snow started coming down I took the last opportunity to get out and meet my friends and get ready for a week of snowball fights. Heyn, Mitiguy, our friend Jon Perkins and me were already in a months-long snowball fight with Perkins's big brother Chris and his friend Monster Rob.

That first morning of the blizzard, we met up in the library parking lot and were quickly set upon by Monster Rob and Big Perkins. About twenty minutes later, we were huddled between the central air-conditioning unit and the building, as we were effectively being destroyed with hard-packed snowballs. We outnumbered them four to two, but they were bigger, and their snowballs stung. We were forced to run, and they followed us all the way up to Shattuck Park, where we were able to hold them off for a while from behind a stone wall—but then they stormed that, and so we ran through several backyards to my house, where they continued to pummel us. As we took fire from behind we ran inside via my basement door and slammed it shut. Snowballs pounded on the door. *BUPH! BUPH!*

But we were safe inside the basement. Soaked and exhausted, we stood in a puddle and breathed easy. Then, two more snowballs hit the door.

We started to laugh.

"What the hell is going on here?!!" Out of the darkness came a sight much more terrifying than any snowball: my father. He was home, totally out of the norm. It was the daytime! But of course it was the Blizzard of '78 and nobody was at work.

"You're dripping everywhere, get the hell out of the cellar!" he shouted.

I shrugged my shoulders and nodded. Physical gestures seemed to work best with my dad; if absolutely necessary, a few mumbled words. I don't think I spoke a complete sentence to him until the mideighties.

BUPH! BUPH . . . BUPH!

"What the hell?" My dad pushed by us and walked to the door. I looked to my friends, as if to ask them if I should stop him. It seemed to happen in slow motion as he reached for the door, turned the knob, and swung it wide open.

BUPH . . . BUPH . . . BUPH!

I was looking at the silhouette of my dad in the doorway as he was bombarded with well-packed Blizzard of '78 snowballs. Through his legs I could see the fierce determination on the faces of these two tough guys as they unloaded their frozen projectiles, then, as they hit the target, I watched their expression turn to shock, then horror, as they realized what they had done. THEY HAD HIT MR. SHILLUE.

Mr. Shillue! The most feared of men! He seemed to enjoy his status as the scariest dad this side of Winter Street. (The south end of Winter Street had a few divorced families on it, and the moms' boyfriends, while technically not dads, were definitely scary and drove vans.)

I stared, savoring the wonderful sight of Monster Rob and Big Perkins struggling through the snow, running in the other direction as fast as they could. My dad was still standing in the doorway in shock as the snow and slush dripped off him. He turned around slowly, slush sliding down the sides of his head.

"GET THE HELL OUT OF HERE!" he yelled at us, as loud as I'd ever heard him.

We scrambled outside and ran until we were out of range of my house. We eventually caught up with Big Perkins and Monster Rob, but instead of starting the fight up again, everyone burst out laughing. We had a solidarity now—we were able to bond over my mean dad.

The Blizzard of '78 had arrived at just the right time in my life. I was at the perfect age to take maximum advantage of its magic. That snowstorm, with the fifteen-foot snowbanks and the reckless abandon with which we took the streets, was pure kid joy, the kind that I'm not sure would ever be possible today.

CHAPTER 10

BE PREPARED

WHEN I WAS TWELVE YEARS OLD I OFFICIALLY became a Boy Scout. As a scout, few things excited me as much as the prospect of going to camp. You noticed I said *camp* and not *sleepaway camp*, a redundant term used by many New York parents. All camps by definition should involve sleeping away. The camps they refer to are not actually camps at all; they are places somewhere deep in Westchester or Long Island with lots of trees, where their kids are shipped in the summer. At a real camp one must, after all, camp. If you have to put the word *sleepaway* in front of your camp, you are probably running a resort.

For years I longed to go out into the woods and do all the things I had read about in the Boy Scout Manual. I had pored over every page of that book, learning everything one needed to know to become an impressive man: knot tying, tent pitching, water collecting, fire building, and, most important, good citizenship (whatever that meant). I would stare for hours at the front cover of the manual, at the pen-and-ink sketch of the teenaged Scout in his pressed khaki uniform striding purposefully toward me, adorned with merit badges that attested to his mastery of many disciplines. *This is the boy,* I thought, *that I am destined to be.*

I could see myself clearly in my mind: piercing the center of the target on the rifle range and being awarded the rifleman badge; demonstrating my ability to spark a flint into a flame and earning my fire starter badge; boiling potatoes with that flame and then proudly collecting my cooking badge. I would fill my shirt with these badges until there was not an inch left, and then I would get a sash to hold the rest.

Troop 49 met in the St. Catherine's church basement and therefore we had a decidedly Catholic slant to our Scouting activities. We all prayed together at the start of meetings, and the only merit badge that everyone in the troop was required to get was the Ad Altare Dei badge.*

Scouts particularly appealed to me because though I loved sports and athletic competitions of all kinds, I was never the best athlete, but I knew I could be the best scout. The only physical conditioning we had to endure at our scout meetings was the painful "duck-walk," which was used as disciplinary tactic when we got out of line. This involved being forced to walk in a deep squat, like a duck, up and down a long hallway in the church basement. We were made to walk like this for a

---

* Ad Altare Dei is the Catholic merit badge. To get it you need to display knowledge and reverence for the Holy Trinity. As badges go, I'd never been more prepared for one.

time that was commensurate with the level of our misbehavior. It may not sound like much, but unless you have done this walk, you should not belittle this punishment technique. The burn in the legs is intense. If I ever have an occasion to interrogate a prisoner, I'm going to use it. It is not torture, but it skirts the line. And so, I did everything I could to avoid being punished at Boy Scout meetings.

But for the most part Troop 49 meetings were lacking in adventure. We watched slide shows about poisonous leaves and berries and old 16mm safety films of all kinds. I suspect that our Scout leader Mr. McCue had access to a massive library of training films in that church basement, which he used whenever he wanted to burn through a few hours of Scout meeting time. I remember once watching a driving safety film—even though for most of us, getting our license was years off—that demonstrated the proper technique for steering a car while sliding on ice.

"Resist the urge to turn the wheel in the opposite direction—this will only increase the lack of control," the narrator said. "It may feel wrong, but turn the wheel *toward the skid*. The wheels will gain traction and then you will once again be able to regain control of the vehicle."

I remember thinking that this advice seemed so counterintuitive that it must be true. I ran over the scenario in my head many times, imagining a time when I might be able to make use of the maneuver, perhaps years later when I had my license and happened to be driving across a frozen lake.

But despite the occasional James Bond driving lessons or duck walks, these weekly meetings in the church did not excite me. I longed for real scouting, out in the wild, with tents and fires. I pictured what it would be like. I would walk into the woods a boy and emerge a man with a coon hide hanging from my waist. What had transpired between the coon and me? Well, they'd just have to use their imaginations. Suffice to say, I was ready to leave the friendly confines of our neighborhood for a month in the woods.

I brought along my Pillsbury Doughboy, a tiny rubber reproduction of the little doughboy that appeared in all the Poppin' Fresh Dough commercials. For years I'd kept him propped against my headboard. Here's the thing—I didn't think of him as a doll, more as a cool mascot. Linus had his blanket, and while he was certainly seen as eccentric, he was by no means a social outcast. And Dwight Stones, the 1972 Olympic high jump champion, used to wear his trademark Mickey Mouse T-shirt to almost every meet. The sports announcers would always mention it, and it was considered quirky and hip. My Pillsbury Doughboy was, I thought, a sign of my offbeat coolness. As I was packing for my trip, I impulsively threw him into the footlocker.

When I arrived at camp, however, and saw the dynamic among the scouts, I quickly got the sense that it would be best to keep my little friend out of sight. I know it's hard to believe, but it seemed the Boy Scouts were bigger ruffians than the choirboys. So in the footlocker he remained.

One thing was for sure, I certainly did not want to end up like the Gaynor Brothers. Tommy and Jimmy Gaynor were the fairest of boys. They had red hair and freckles the color of cantaloupe, their skin was so light it had an almost translucent quality to it. On sunny days you could actually see right through it and into their bodies. I distinctly remember watching Jimmy on the dock one late afternoon, cautiously dipping his toe in to test the water. With the sun low in the sky behind him, I swear I could clearly see the internal organs sloshing around beneath his soft exterior, and the veins and arteries pulsing blood to and from his heart, blue going in, red going out. He looked like an out-of-shape version of the Slim Good-body exhibit at the Museum of Science in Boston.

Everybody always gave the Gaynor Brothers a hard time. Their name, after all, did them no favors. That kind of stacked the deck against them. At some point in the family line you'd think someone would have had the decency to move a few letters around and thereby prevent future generations having to endure the teasing. It might also have been useless, since young boys have an uncanny ability to re-anagram any name at all into a homosexual slur, but with Gaynor, you are really handing it to them on a silver platter.

As expected, the Brothers had to leave camp early. Their mother was forced to pick them up halfway through the month because they could not stand the name-calling. At least that's what the scout leaders told Mrs. Gaynor. "There's a lot of razzing going on here. It just got to be a little much for the boys," they said.

In reality, the scout leaders were doing their share of the razzing. Older Eagle Scouts who volunteered as camp counselors taught some of the merit badge courses. On the archery range, one of these counselors drew his bow back as far as possible and announced "This is what you should never do!" and shot an arrow toward the horizon. Then he turned to Tommy Gaynor and said, "Go get that." Tommy ran off, and all the scouts (including me) began to snicker. When he returned ten minutes later, sunburned and mottled with wasp bites, the scoutmaster said, "And never do this!" Then he turned and fired an arrow deep into the woods. "Go get that!" Off Tommy ran again, toward certain Lyme disease. Everybody could tell which side the scout leaders were on.

With the Gaynors gone, I knew their tormentors would look around for low-hanging fruit to pick on, so I made sure to keep on my toes. I thought I was doing just fine until one night when I was going through my footlocker my tent mate Danny said, "What's that?"

"Doughboy," I said, as offhandedly as possible. "Got it free because I ate a ton of crescent rolls," I added with a laugh.

Danny didn't say anything else, but I knew that I should remain on alert. It was hard to tell how he'd play the situation. He could immediately tell the other scouts or hold the information for a later date. Ready for anything, I went to sleep.

I didn't have to wait long. I awoke to the sound of laughter outside my tent. The sound of laughter at Boy Scout camp can only mean one thing: someone is being victimized. I pulled back the canvas flap and saw a circle of boys about twenty yards away. I pulled on my pants without even bothering to shake out the spiders and stepped outside to see what all the fun was about. As I walked closer to the circle, I could see they all had their scout knives out. Then, briefly, I saw him, pierced on the end of a knife like a marshmallow. They were tossing my Pillsbury Doughboy from one knife to the next.

They were all participating, even Michael Madero, the Eagle Scout with mild cerebral palsy. They saw me approach the circle, but continued on, intent on keeping the knife-toss game going. It wasn't much of a game, really—the Doughboy was not ideally suited for tossing cleanly from one knife to the next. Mostly one boy would thrust it at another boy, who would try to stab it and fail, then it would fall to the ground and the boy would place it on the knife and hurl it on to the next. This is the way it went, on and on, as the scouts waited for me to do the inevitable: run into the circle and scream in protest.

"Be Prepared" was the Scout Motto. I took it to heart. As I walked toward them, I made sure there was a smile on my face. I pulled out my scout knife, opened it slowly as I edged into the circle . . . and joined in the stabbing. I stabbed my own Doughboy with a spirited energy, laughing along with them as they stomped on him and stabbed him again and again.

Stabbing him came easily to me. It reminded me of when I was very young and Joey Reichart flipped my plastic swimming pool over and began kicking it with his heel. He put his foot through it and laughed. I laughed, too, and did the same thing. Then we each took turns kicking holes in my pool. By the time we were done, the entire bottom was covered with heel-shaped chads. "Why did you do that?" my mother asked as she was putting the pool out on the curb with the rest of the trash. I had no answer for her. I liked the pool. But I suppose it was preferable to join in and help destroy your property than to stand there crying while someone else did.

Soon Doughboy was dirtied and covered in lacerations. His head was coming off and hanging to the side. When he arrived on my knife again, I decided I should be the one to bring this morbid event to a close. I opened up his side with my knife, scooped in a bunch of dirt and rocks to fill him with a good bit of weight, and then hurled him into the lake. That was it. It was over.

The scouts folded up their knives and began to disperse. Michael Madero looked at me with what appeared to be a smirk (it was sometimes hard to tell with the cerebral palsy) and nodded as if to say, "Not bad, kid. Not bad at all." I had handled it perfectly. This would be the last razzing I got from them, and I'd escaped with barely a scrape. I certainly wasn't going to end up like the Gaynor Brothers. I had passed the test and turned the skidding car in the direction of the skid, righting the vehicle.

I got halfway up the hill to the mess hall when, like Lot's wife, I turned and looked back to the lake. To my surprise, there he was, my doll, looking back at me. At that moment he was a doll, not some cool mascot. He had spent years resting on my headboard, and I liked his face. His little chef's hat had filled with air, creating buoyancy, and he bobbed up and down on the water. He looked at me with that permanent smile of his affixed to his face. Did he understand? Was he at peace with what happened? Or behind that smile was he thinking, *Why, Tommy? Why'd you do it? I thought we were friends.*

The lapping water seemed to wash away his wounds, which appeared less mortal now, as he floated along cheerfully. My impulse was to run down the hill, jump in, and swim to him, but I would not. I could not. He had to be sacrificed so that I could flourish.

I turned and walked into the mess hall. Everybody had a laugh about it over breakfast. And later that night in the main tent, I showed them how to make a moth disoriented by pulling out its antennae. It was something one of the Eagle Scouts had shown me in forestry class. As the big moth bounced off the floor and my fellow scouts laughed and hooted, I knew the next few weeks of camp would be just fine.

Camp, like the neighborhood, was a place where violence

and fear were staples. It was not the kind of violence that would leave you really hurt, though, only your pride. It was *Lord of the Flies* every day back then. It was tough, but if you handled it the right way, it made you more resilient. I wonder if my kids could take it. I wonder if I would let them.

CHAPTER 11

BE REVERENT

I WAS AN ALTAR BOY AT ST. CATHERINE OF SIENNA PAR-
ish. It was either become an altar boy or join the choirboys,
so I went with the less risky choice. The choirboys were the
tougher of the two groups, although most people would probably expect it would be the other way around. I think the reason was that the choirboys rehearsed all together in one big
group, which is a formula for rank pulling and macho postur-
ing of all sorts. There are many opportunities for bullying in
a choir. The basses and baritones tend to be the older boys,
so they exerted a natural dominance over the higher ranges.
But hazing and intimidation really only happened among the
second-stringers, the minions. The top soloists were immune
because they were too talented to mess with, so they operated
in a separate, safe space. All in all, there was just way too much
jockeying for position in the choir for my taste.

We altar boys only mixed with the choirboys when we rehearsed together before special Masses like Christmas and Easter, or for the occasional group outings.

We once went on a combined altar boy/choirboy field trip to the Stoneham Zoo, which is about an hour's ride from Norwood, and as soon as we got on the bus one of the big baritones shouted, "Choirboys in back only, altar boys in the front!" (We are all aware, because we learned in our civil rights history, that "back of the bus" was where the oppressed had to sit, but clearly nobody told adolescent boys: to them the back of the bus is always the desirable place to be.) But the altar boys didn't even object; we sat in the front and let the choirboys have their preferred seats, with the toughest ones huddled by the emergency exit, where they could moon cars when we pulled out onto the highway. We didn't make a fuss, we knew who was who. Those guys spent the whole Mass in the organ loft. We were front-of-the-house guys, and had to act accordingly. And I was just fine with that. In fact, I loved being an altar boy, because ours was a culture of comradery. We needed to stick together and look out for one another, whether against nosey nuns or the ever-grumpy monsignor. (I had great respect and an easygoing rapport with most of the priests, but the tall, menacing monsignor at St. Catherine's, with his slicked back head of Brylcreem and permanent scowl, was never fun to work with.)

As an altar boy you were mostly working two per Mass, so it was easier to get along. If you were paired with an older boy, he'd be the dominant one, but since there was no one else around to see the dominance, he wouldn't bother taking advantage of it. He'd just take the better jobs—you'd wash the glass fonts, he'd fill them with water and wine. He'd light the candles before Mass, and you had to put them out after. But if you're working with someone one-on-one, it's hard not to get along.

Whenever Andy French, a friend of mine from school, and I would serve Mass together, we'd have so much fun, daring each other with bell-ringing contests during Mass. If you've been to more than a few Catholic Masses, you know where the bells come in. During transubstantiation, the bread and wine is being transformed into Jesus' body and blood, and it's time for a little wake-up call to the congregation.

"It shall be shed for you and for all men so that sins may be forgiven. Do this in memory of me." (Ring!)

There is no set time for how long the ringing is supposed to go on; it's left up to the discretion of the altar boy. Andy French and I would have contests to see who could ring the longest. The priest would lift the brass chalice aloft and wait for the ringing to stop, and we'd just keep ringing and ringing. Sometimes the priest would shoot us a look, and we'd quickly muffle the bells onto the red velvet pillow. After the look, it was game over. (We did this with any priest but the monsignor, of course, who scared the hell out of both of us.)

As a new altar boy you had to start by serving at daily Mass, which is like when you get a job waiting tables and you have to take the lunch shifts nobody wants. Sunday Masses were like dinner shifts; you had to work up to them. And the most coveted, the Friday-night dinner shifts of Masses, were weddings. You got tipped at a wedding Mass. (Sometimes you got tips at a funeral Mass too, but you didn't expect it. You always got a tip at a wedding.) It was an amazing feeling when someone stuffed a $20 bill in your hand after serving Mass, though it almost seemed wrong. But of course I stuffed it right in my pocket; I wasn't going to argue with Sacramental Tradition.

The 5:15 p.m. daily Masses, however, were a grind. They took place in the chapel behind the church. It had all the same ornate detailing of the church, but in a more intimate space, with just ten rows of pews. With the late-afternoon sunlight beaming through the stained-glass windows, washing the miniature altar in colored light, my every move was exposed. I could barely see the pews in the darkness, but I knew they were filled with mostly old ladies and nuns who knew every second of the Mass by heart. With them, the slightest error would be noticed—it was like having to perform a jazz recital in front of Miles Davis and Charlie Parker.

The chief job of the altar boy was dealing with the priest's Mass book, a massive tome that you were required to carry through the church behind the priest at the start of Mass. Once on the altar, you had to place it on the wooden stand in front of the priest, then open to the correct page. It was very intimidating at first: there were several pages to be turned during the Mass, but they were clearly marked with ribbons, so once you learned the proper order it was not too difficult. If you did make a mistake and opened to the wrong page, the priest would simply grab hold of a different ribbon and open to the correct section. They probably shouldn't have trusted this task to the altar boys in the first place, because obviously the priest was much more familiar with the Mass book than we were. I guess it was, like most of our duties, an exercise in making us pay attention.

But in the chapel there was no book stand. When it was time to read, the altar boy had to *become* a book stand. You had to stand and turn to face the priest, then clean and jerk the magnum opus up to your forehead, holding this position while he read from it. The priest was two steps up, so my method was to put one foot on the lowest step and one on the higher one, as it helped with balance. Oddly enough, this book-balancing act made me the least nervous of all my duties. It seemed so dated and courtly, and I knew it was ridiculous for the Church to expect anyone to be good at this. If a boy were to slip and the whole thing came toppling down, most reasonable people in attendance would have to split the blame between the boy and Rome.

At one of my first daily Masses I had forgotten to wear black shoes; I still had my high-top sneakers on from school. These were a no-no—it said right there in the altar boys' guide: *"Remember, you are in the presence of Christ when you are stepping upon the altar—dress for the occasion!"*

At the time I was less worried about Christ than my immediate superiors. The sneakers had gotten past Father Curran in the sacristy, but he was the most laid back of all the priests at St. Catherine's, with the encouraging demeanor of a basketball coach. He had a thick head of white hair, black eyebrows, and a nose that looked, as he described it, like it was stuffed full of nickels. "Wouldn't you like to have a nose this this? Stuffed full of nickels?" he'd always say, as if we understood the reference. It would be thirty-five years before I found out he was quoting W. C. Fields.

He'd sit with us before Mass and ask about school and sports, and whether we were holding hands yet with any girls.

"You like any girls at school?"

"Yeah, maybe."

"You holding hands yet?"

"No, not yet."

"Nothing wrong with holding hands with them after school. Holding hands . . . it's a beautiful thing. Yep. That's all, though! Remember that."

"OK."

"Nothing wrong with holding hands."

Some might see something inappropriate in this exchange, but I assure you it wasn't at all. In fact, I was relieved that a member of the clergy was giving me the green light on romance of any kind. I took it as encouragement, and when it did come time for me to attempt some aggressive hand holding with a girl, I gave credit to Father Curran.

There was no organ music in the chapel, so the sound of every footstep on the marble altar, and the lightest *ping* on the brass chalice could be heard by everyone. Sister Coleen, the sternest of all the nuns, was in the front row. I could just see her eyelids and nose from beneath the shadow of her habit. I wondered if she had spied my blasphemous footwear. When I was sitting I was fine, I could slide them behind me. But when I was standing, anyone could see the rubber soles sticking out from the bottom of my cassock, so during the Mass I was trying to bend slightly at the knees to bring the black hem down just enough to cover the front of them. As a result, when I walked I had to shuffle noisily across the altar—and sneakers on marble make a telltale squeak. I was on a razor's edge—I could be given away at any second by the sight of my high-top or that horrible sound.

While trying to maintain my slight squat, I must have leaned a little too much to the left and gotten the large arm of my white surplus over one of the candles at the side of the altar. In seconds it caught fire.* I hadn't seen it, but Sister Coleen had. Her eyelids flipped up to reveal two icy eyes and

---

* Altar boys have two vestments, the cassock, which is the long black robe that goes on the inside, and the surplus, which is the loose-fitting white top that's worn over it.

a pursed expression that said, "Take care of that right this in-stant!" I looked down and pulled my arm away quickly, but my surplus was aflame. I couldn't cause a scene because everyone knows you can't just stop a Mass because you've got a personal problem. So I tried to lightly shake the fire out. I repeated that a few times, but the flame only got bigger. As the instinct to remain alive suddenly overtook my desire to behave myself, I picked up my other arm and flapped repeatedly at the fire with the palm of my hand. The surplus must have been made with a somewhat flame-retardant material because after a few slaps the fire went out, and a tuft of smoke rose into the air.* The scent of beeswax was replaced by that of burnt polyester.

Father Curran stopped speaking but kept his palms facing up as he looked over at me.

"Everything all right over there?" he asked, calmly.

I could hear the gasps from the pews.

"Yep. It's OK," I said quietly.

Father Curran continued. I looked from my crispy uni-form down to the front pew, and God's personal secretary Sis-ter Coleen was looking me over. She wasn't concerned with my safety. She wasn't even looking at the hole I'd burnt in my vest-ments. She was looking at my high-tops. My carelessness had interrupted Mass, and it all started because I hadn't shown the proper respect by wearing a nice pair of dress shoes. Well, at the very least, I knew I had something for confession that week besides "I fought with my brothers and sisters."

Whenever I mention that I was an altar boy, people like

---

* As it should have been. Think about it: you've got young boys wrapped in copious amounts of loose fabric walking among candles. Our vest-ments should have looked more like HASMAT suits.

to ask, "Did you hit that altar wine?" Everyone seems to have heard stories of altar boys getting drunk on the Communion stash. It's not surprising; entrusting the keys to a closet full of wine jugs to young boys almost guarantees underage intoxication. Almost. I never once took a sip. For me, this was far too obvious a crime. The fact that we were trusted not to do this—and that it would have been so easy to pour out a mugful, or to take a swig from a jug any time we wanted, made me never want to do it. I had a responsibility, and I took it seriously. So, I'm sorry, I don't have any stories about getting drunk on bad Communion wine.

That's not to say that I was the perfect altar boy. I've already mentioned the bell-ringing contests and the sneaker incident. I engaged in more innocent misbehavior with my main altar boy pal Andy French. After the 5:15 p.m. Mass in the main church, we'd have to turn off all the lights and close down the church. In the winter months, it got dark early, so there was no light at all coming in through the stained-glass windows. As we went about our job of shutting down the lights, the church would become a sea of darkness. Total blackness. And that's when Andy and I would have races: from the back of the church to the front, in the wide middle aisle, we'd run our fastest fifty-yard dash in complete darkness. (If you've never done it, it's surprisingly terrifying to run at top speed without being able to see where you are going.) Then we'd go up on the altar and try to walk around, playing the game of "first person to bump into something loses." This would always end with something loudly tumbling over and clanging onto the marble altar, making an enormous racket. We'd fall to the floor laughing for several minutes, listening to ourselves echo through the church. In retrospect it all sounds fairly innocent, but at the time it felt like the most cardinal of sins. We were horsing around in God's house. It was disrespectful, and we knew it, which is why it was fun. I would ask forgiveness when I said my prayers, assuring God that I only did it because Andy was with me, and I'm sure Andy said the same about me. But we'd both do it again. And we were sure that God forgave us.

CHAPTER 12

BE A GENTLEMAN

AS I MOVED INTO MY DOUBLE DIGITS AND THEN early-teen years, new interests and issues started to creep into my world—trying to look cool; what kind of car we were going to get when we could drive; the fact that people drank and did illegal things like drugs to have a good time; rock music, which was pretty great; and girls, who might be somewhat interesting. Of course, my friends and I were still a few years away from really getting into any of these things, and some would argue that we never pulled off the looking-cool part. But this was the time that these ideas started to seep into our consciousness, and along with that came a slightly different sense of vigilance from our parents that often led to some cringe-inducing conversations. Now, kids just learn everything from the Internet by the time they get to middle school.

One such occasion involved the now classic album *Bat Out of Hell* by everyone's favorite rock star named for a food item, Meat Loaf. I didn't go out and buy that album, but it sure found its way into my life. I had offered to help Heyn babysit for his sister, and his brother-in-law was blasting Meat Loaf on the stereo when we went over to his house after school. I recall not liking it all that much when I first heard it.

"You like Meat Loaf?" he yelled at us. "Oh, this album's great—you gotta listen to this!"

He turned up the volume on the wailing, plaintive ballad— *I want you, I need you* . . .

Heyn and I sat and listened to the album as his brother-in-law got ready to go out. I remember him standing in the bathroom with the door open blow-drying his hair and his mustache. When he was done, he appeared in the living room in tight jeans and a silky piratelike shirt; he checked himself out in the full-length mirror, fluffing the long hair behind his ears with his fingers. He then took what appeared to be a giant water-filled test-tube off the mantel, held a lighter to it, and began sucking smoke through the top. The smoke smelled sweet like manure, and when he was done sucking he held his breath for several seconds. What kind of science experiment was this? Then he gave us some final instructions.

"There's vood in the vridge! Stereo's all yours!" he said through his teeth, still holding the smoke in.

Next, Heyn's brother-in-law walked out on the porch and exhaled the smoke into the cold air as he went down the stairs. *Was he holding his breath so he wouldn't get smoke in his house? Then why would he have a massive smoke apparatus on the mantel?* I knew there must be something illicit to this ritual of his, because I had never seen it done before. Most things that were OK to do were either done by your parents or done on TV shows. For instance, my parents drank beer and wine but never hard liquor like bourbon and gin. But I knew drinking bourbon and gin wasn't illegal because I'd watched it on shows like *A Family Affair* and *M*A*S*H*. I looked forward to the day when I would drink hard liquor, because it was clearly something sophisticated people did, even though it was tinged with a bit of danger, too. I remember watching the film *Mr. Roberts*, which takes place on a WWII supply ship in the Pacific. There is a scene in which Henry Fonda, William Powell, and Jack Lemmon attempt to whip up an emergency batch of scotch in anticipation of a visit from a team of nurses. They mix together rubbing alcohol, Coca-Cola, and iodine. As each of them samples the finished product, they wince, cough, and then say, "Wow. That's good stuff!"

So what was this mysterious concoction that provided both pain and pleasure? I wanted to know. Heyn's brother-in-law's ritual seemed, like the *Mr. Roberts* scene, to be both pleasant and unpleasant at the same time.

It's not surprising that it was Heyn's brother-in-law who was the person who introduced me to *Bat Out of Hell*. Meat Loaf also seemed to be trafficking in forbidden fruit. The cover featured a demonlike motorcycle rider blasting up from beneath the earth of a cemetery plot (fresh from a visit to, apparently, Hell). It was foreboding imagery. The songs, too, seemed off-putting and aggressive, but due to the high recommendation of his brother-in-law, Johnny Heyn bought the Meat Loaf album. He played it at his house for weeks, and some of the songs eventually began to grow on me. When I told Heynzy that I might be becoming a Meat Loaf fan, he immediately offered to sell me the album.

"Give me five dollars for it," he said.

I hedged. "Why do you want to get rid of it?"

"I need the money. Give me four dollars."

I certainly didn't like the album enough to want to own it, but four dollars seemed to be a pretty good price. A new album went for twice that much.

It wasn't until I was actually in possession of the album that I realized it could be a problem. Not only did the cover art suggest demonic activity, but the back of the album featured a photo of Meat Loaf and his "band," a woman whom he appeared to be groping, and another guy who seemed to be up to *no good at all*. I hid the album under my jacket when I went home and buried it in my closet.

One day I was going down to the cellar to get some canned goods, trying as usual not to make any noise on the stairs as I walked so as not to disturb my father, when out of the shadows my dad appeared.

"Tommy, c'mon in heah," he said.

There was usually something fun about being called into my dad's cigar smoke-filled office. Despite worrying about the potentially terrible conversation that might follow, it was fascinating to see what was going on in there. My dad worked in the exciting new field of computer programming, so the room was filled with stacks of programming books, reams of the green and white zigzag printer paper with the holes on one side, and boxes of large reel-to-reel disks, which stored something called data.

He also wrote poetry, and had several pads of legal paper on which he would write page after page of rhyming verse. I would always try to sneak looks at the poetry as my dad was lecturing me. I don't remember doing any of that at this meeting, however. This meeting with my dad would be the most awkward ever.

I sat down on a box of computer paper next to him and immediately noticed the Meat Loaf *Bat Out of Hell* album on his desk. Of course, what was I thinking? Certainly my mother had found the album while rummaging through my closet one day and turned it over to him. The record was out of its sheath, and in my dad's hand was the record sleeve, which featured all of the lyrics to Meat Loaf's songs.

Now, I have to address Mr. Loaf directly here: Why did you include the song lyrics within your album? You must have known your target demographic was suburban youth with strict parents who would inevitably snoop into their bedrooms and find the lyrics, leading to conversations like this:

"Is this yaw reckud album?"

"Yeah."

"Whea'd you get it?"

"Bought it from Johnny Heyn."

"We'll, you may want to get yaw money back."

"Oh."

"You think this guy is a good musician?"

"I just like the guitars."

"You think this is an ahtist? 'Paradise by the Dashboard Light'? You agree with this viewpoint?"

"I don't think so."

He began to read aloud. He proceeded to read all the lyrics aloud, slowly and deliberately, occasionally pausing to ask things like, "You concur with this type of sentiment?"

"No. I don't think so."

"*We're gonna go all the way tonight, tonight.* Could you tell me what that means?"

"I just like the beat. Of the drums."

I was just looking for something to say so he would stop reading the lyrics to me.

My dad parsed the whole album, song by song, occasionally pausing to see if I would help him interpret a passage.

Clearly, Mr. Shillue was no fan of Mr. Loaf. He had no desire whatsoever for his son Tommy to be filling his head with the imagery of his songcraft. And after hearing my dad describe all that sexual longing out loud with a heavy Boston accent, I was ready to become a monk and take a vow of celibacy.

Needless to say, I took the album back to Heyn. He refused to give me my four dollars back, but I told him to keep it anyway.

"I'll play it for you when you come over," said Heyn.

"No, thanks. I'm sick of it," I said. Those songs would never be the same after the dramatic reading my father had given them.

To this day, if I'm in a café or a mall and one of the songs from the *Bat Out of Hell* starts playing, I can hear only the voice of my dad.

"Now, whattaya think theyah getting at here? Is this the kind of behaviah somebody should try and emulate?"

*

Heyn and I were riding our bikes around Karen Barker's block. When we passed her house we'd slow down and do some donuts opposite each other, talking loudly as we circled, then continue around again. Karen Barker had a pool in her backyard, and we were bucking for an invite. We couldn't have been more obvious if we'd been wearing snorkel masks and fins, but we thought we were being subtle.

After several laps around the block we came around the corner and Karen was out on the lawn. Casually, we stopped our bikes to talk. We'd known Karen since the second grade. She was always one of the smartest, prettiest girls in the class.

We talked about school and who our teachers were going to be come September. After fifteen minutes of small talk she finally asked the million-dollar question: "Do you guys want to come swim in my pool?"

Heynzy and I looked at each other like we had to think about our decision. It was the same faux nonchalance that my brother and I exhibited when my dad offered to stop at McDonald's. I spent my whole childhood faking a lack of enthusiasm for things I was absolutely ecstatic about.

"Okay." We shrugged. "We'll have to go home and put our suits on."

Since the whole thing was very deliberate, we really should have had our suits on under our cut-off shorts, but we didn't want to appear too eager. We really considered ourselves masters of the low-key approach.

After skidding into my driveway I dropped my bike and ran up the stairs into my bedroom. I fumbled through my drawers until I found my bathing suit and slid it on. I was putting on my sneakers when my dad came in my room.

"Where you headed?" he asked.

"I'm going to swim in Karen Barker's pool."

He sat down on the end of my bed and patted the mattress twice with his hand—the signal for "sit down, we'll have a talk." There must've been something in the way I had pulled in on my bike and ran up the stairs that my dad could sense the excitement in my step. There was no other explanation for his impromptu visit. These father-son talks were rare and always brief. But given how excited I was to get over to Karen Barker's, I was eager to get this one over with. Plus, I had no idea what he wanted to talk about.

I listened to him breathing and waited for him to begin. Finally he broke the silence.

"You know how to deal with women?" he asked. I was surprised by this question. I hadn't done anything to indicate that my swimming endeavor had anything to do with "women," as my dad had put it. It also didn't seem like the kind of question that required an answer from me, so I waited for his. "Smile at 'em," he said. "Just smile at 'em."

"OK," I said.

"That's all you gotta remember. No matter what they do— smile at 'em."

I looked up at my dad. He put his hand on my back and showed me all his teeth, and with a wide-eyed expression, like a ventriloquist's dummy, he repeated it once more for good measure, through the grin: "Smile at 'em!"

I nodded my head, as if I fully comprehended, but as with most of my dad's advice, I'd spend years sorting it all out. With that, he got up and left my bedroom. That was all I was going to get. My dad was famously frugal with language, but on this occasion he outperformed his own reputation for brevity. This would be the only "birds and bees" talk I'd ever get, although at the time, I didn't know it was that at all. I had absolutely no idea why my father was giving me this strange smiling lesson, and I was as uncomfortable as I had been during the dreaded

Meat Loaf conversation, but eventually I saw the value in that talk.

But again, I think it was intentional. My dad would probably have been a great ad copywriter, such was his ability to boil down a big idea into a few words. The phrase "Just Do It" can mean almost anything, but in the context of what we know about the products Nike makes, and the people who use them, the phrase is loaded with meaning about physically going the distance and pushing beyond one's limits.

"Smile at 'em," in the context of my life, and knowing my dad, contained so much more than just the meaning of those words.

Actually, the full extent of my sex education was probably the two bits of advice I received from my dad and Father Curran: "Smile at 'em," and "Just hold hands." There was a great deal of intention and substance in both of the phrases. *Women are important . . . women are special . . . women should be handled carefully . . . be kind . . . be a gentleman . . . go after what you want, but don't push too hard . . . don't overthink things . . . don't be cool . . . less is more . . . play the long game . . . be open . . . be gentle . . . be unafraid.*

The message from my dad that day was also aspirational. I knew that sex was a thing, and knew I was at that stage of life where girls were soon going to be more than a mystery. I knew that on *Happy Days*, Ralph and Potsy went up to Inspiration Point to "neck" with girls and I knew that stage was coming for me, too. As far as learning about sex, there would be other things I would be exposed to, of course: *Playboy*s that were stashed in the woods, and "the books" that were passed around at Boy Scout camp, but those were just the dirty details. There were no lessons in those things. Education is about applying knowledge.

I applied the advice from Dad and Father Curran over and over again, eventually. Smile at 'em became my icebreaker, and holding hands was my key move. I used them on every girl I ever went after. And I'd give the same advice to any young man to this day. These moves work! The smile beats the brooding look, or the dis, or the playful shove, or anything else that teen boys try on a girl. And hand holding, which is never attempted unless you're already on solid ground, is so much better than an arm around the shoulder. You can elicit a response almost immediately when you take a lady's hand, and if you get a squeeze in return, you're on cloud nine. Trust me, young man, you know where you stand with the hand, and it is a gentlemanly way to find out.

CHAPTER 13

BE YOURSELF

WOULD YOU GO TO BED WITH FARAH FAWCETT?" asked Mitiguy.

We were in Heyn's backyard doing what we were always doing: working on a fort.

"What? No. Wait. Why?" I said.

"You wouldn't go to bed with Farah Fawcett?"

"What are you talking about? Why would I do that?" I asked.

The guys giggled.

When it came to girls, I was a little behind Heyn and Mitiguy, and probably most of the guys that were headed to seventh grade along with me that fall.

Sure, I knew that Farah Fawcett was pretty; I stared at the poster of her in the red bathing suit all the time. It was hanging everywhere in the '70's (not in my home, of course, but everywhere else).* I just didn't understand all this talk about going "to bed." It seemed an odd thing to want to do with a girl. I certainly would not have passed up the opportunity to spend an afternoon with Farah Fawcett, or someone like her. Truth be told I was more partial to Christy McNichol from *Family* or Erin from *The Waltons*. If I could get one of them alone for the afternoon, I knew exactly what I would do—take her straight to the Paragon Park amusement park on Nantasket Beach. We'd skip the rides and take a walk together, share some cotton candy, and discuss what the second installment of *Star Wars* was going to include. But that's where my G-rated fantasy ended—sitting on the rocks of a distant jetty and talking until dusk with the sun setting in a sea of beautiful colors and the Ferris wheel slowly turning behind us. That was my idea of perfection. What was all this talk about "bed" anyway? I just had no clue.

"You haven't made out with anyone, have you, Shillue?" said Heyn.

"No, not yet."

"We've got to get you a girl to make out with," he said, like a doctor diagnosing a patient.

"Yeah," agreed Mitiguy, "You've got to have a make-out session. You need to get some experience. I had a make-out session with Mike Doherty's cousin last summer in a hammock, and it was easy. You've got to do it."

"You made out with Mike's cousin?" Heyn asked.

"Yeah. We made out in the hammock for the whole afternoon. It was the same as going to bed."

---

* The iconic picture of Farah Fawcett is the best-selling pinup poster of all time, with more than 12 million copies sold.

"Maybe we can get her to make out with him next time she comes," suggested Heyn, pointing at me.

"No, she won't come until the end of August, and when she does I'm going to make out with her again."

"What about MacPhail?"

"Yeah, good idea. Definitely. MacPhail will do it."

Linda MacPhail. She was tall and pretty and seemed older than the other girls in our class, even though she was the same exact age. But it was really just because she carried herself with a lot of confidence. She had no problem talking with the boys, and this, combined with her good looks, made her seem dangerous. I sure didn't think she would want to have a make-out session with me, even one arranged for purely educational purposes. Did people even do such things? Heyn and Mitiguy had seemed so matter-of-fact about the whole thing, as if it happened all the time.

"I don't know," I said hesitantly.

"Don't worry about it," said Mitiguy. "MacPhail is really advanced. She wears tampons, you know."

"She does?" asked Heyn.

"Yeah, since Play Day last year."

The boys at school had some story they were always whispering to one another, about MacPhail having to leave Play Day because her shorts were stained or something—I didn't want to know a thing about it.

"I'm gonna call her and ask her to have a make-out session with Shillue. She'll do it. I know it."

The following day Mitiguy told me he had arranged my make-out session with Linda MacPhail for that Saturday afternoon. It was to take place behind the Star Market, in the recycling bin, an 18-wheeler tractor trailer container that was filled with stacks of newspaper bundles.

The recycling bin, with its many crevices and hiding places, was the perfect place for clandestine meetings. We had gone there once to divvy up the loot from a parking meter that Mitiguy had managed to break open using a loose cobblestone. The booty seemed huge, but I was a little uncomfortable with the way in which it had been acquired. Picking loose coins from a parking meter, which we did all the time, was one thing, but the cobblestone ratcheted it up into "illegal" territory. Since I had felt guilty about it, I didn't want to just go out and splurge with the money. My idea was to bury all the money in the woods and, as the years went by, add to the stash little by little (not with other stolen money, but earnings from legit endeavors). Eventually we could use the accumulated fortune to pay for a trip to Florida after we graduated from high school. Heyn and Mitiguy thought we should immediately take the money to the Ground Round and use it to play Atari Games for the rest of the afternoon. They prevailed. A few hours after the parking meter heist, all the coins were gone, and all three of us were suffering from carpel tunnel syndrome from excessive track ball use.

"Does MacPhail know it's me she's going to be making out with?" I asked.

"She knows everything. I explained your situation," said Mitiguy.

I didn't even know what my situation was. *Why did I need special attention? Just because I didn't agree that the best use of one's time is to languor in bed all day with Farah Fawcett?* I did, however, go along with the project. As intimidated and as confused as I was, I was thrilled by the idea of making out with Linda

MacPhail in the recycling bin. And I couldn't pass up the shot at a free lesson. I've always had a great lust for learning.

"What should I do first?" I asked.

"Don't worry about it. She'll know what to do. She's advanced."

I didn't ask Mitiguy what he meant, as it was probably all bluster. If he knew so much, why wasn't he going to make out with her? I wasn't sure if I was getting set up for a disappointment, or a prank, or worse. But I forged ahead.

So on the fateful day, I pulled up to the recycling bin on my Schwinn. I could see MacPhail's ten-speed already leaning against the side. I put my bike alongside hers and climbed inside. The air inside was hot and thick, nearly unbearable.

"Hello?" I said.

"I'm back here," I heard from behind the stacks.

I climbed up a steep hill of newspapers, across a short plateau, and then down a slight ravine to the back of the container, where Linda MacPhail was waiting. She was leaning against the wall of the container with her knees up to her chest, and had a newspaper behind her back to protect her from the scorching metal wall. She was wearing white jeans and a tank top.

I was wearing a cotton football jersey with three-quarter-length sleeves and a pair of Sears Toughskins, those blue jeans that have rectangular plates of space age material stitched into both knees.

Why am I still wearing Toughskins? I thought to myself. *I've got to get a pair of regular blue jeans.* Even J.C. Penney Plain Pockets had a higher status than Toughskins. She looked like she was seventeen. I looked like I was seven.

"Hi," she said.

"How you doing?" I asked.

"Good."

"You reading any newspapers?" I joked.

"Not yet," she said, laughing.

"Are you going to play soccer this summer at Father Mac's?"

"I think so."

We talked about school and Father Mac's playground for a bit, and my nervousness began to evaporate. I told her the story of our parking meter heist, and how we'd blown it all on video games; I complained about Heyn and Mitiguy for a while, and she complained about some of her girlfriends. After about half an hour, both of us were pretty well soaked with sweat, and Linda suggested that we should probably go outside. We crawled up and out of the bin, and when we got outside I noticed that her white jeans had black newsprint stains all over them. I didn't say anything about the stains. The palms of my hands were black, too. It felt freezing cold outside, even thought it was late June, and probably in the eighties.

"You wanna go for a bike ride?" she asked.

"Sure."

As I pulled on my bike, hers came with it. My pedal was stuck between the spokes of her wheel, and I had to pry my Schwinn carefully apart from her ten-speed. Our bikes had been more intimate than we had.

We rode up to St. Timothy's Church parking lot, which overlooked New Pond. It was a great spot. I made up for my lack of a ten-speed by popping a few wheelies and doing some hot-dogging moves that could only be done on a two-wheeler with regular handlebars. At one point I got off my bike and chased the ducks into the water, which made her laugh.

"You're weird!" she said.

I liked that.

It was late in the afternoon when I rode with her back to her house, and we said good-bye without getting off our bikes. Neither of us had mentioned the original purpose of our meeting. But as I rode home, I remember thinking the day had gone pretty perfectly, even without the jetty and the Ferris wheel in the background. When Heyn and Mitiguy asked, I decided I would just tell them that we had made out and leave it at that. Nobody had to know the truth, and I didn't want to spoil the good day I had with Linda by telling them.

But she had laughed and said I was weird, which stuck with me. Maybe I'd be the weird guy. Maybe that would be my thing.

CHAPTER 14

BE BOLD

NOTHING EPITOMIZED MY 1950S CHILDHOOD IN THE 1970s as much as Roll-Land, an old-fashioned roller rink that had operated for generations and remained largely unchanged from its earliest days. It was housed in an airplane hanger–sized building along "Automile" on Route 1 at the edge of town.*

Roll-Land promised, as a banner inside proclaimed, "Leisure, Fun and Wholesome Recreation for the Whole Family" but Friday nights belonged to the junior high set. As young teens we would gather to skate, but mostly to socialize, and experience our first, tenuous interactions with the opposite

---

* A large cluster of automobile dealerships on Route 1 is known as the Norwood "Automile," almost all of which were owned by Ernie Boch, famous in the Boston area for his TV commercials urging people to "Come on down!"

sex. Raised up in a loft at the corner of the big wooden rink was a live organist who would accompany the skating on his Mighty Wurlitzer, playing everything from "Let Me Call You Sweetheart" to "Toot, Toot, Tootsie! (Good-bye)." That's right, the entire Hit Parade. One side of the rink had turquoise melamine benches, and the other side had a snack bar that served burgers, dogs, pizza slices, and fountain sodas. Along the wall next to the snack bar was a line of pinball machines, which were usually monopolized by a group of toughs that looked like they were straight out of S. E. Hinton's *The Outsiders*. There was a big sign on the wall that lit up skating commands, like ALL SKATE, COUPLES ONLY, RHUMBA, CHA CHA, and BOSSA NOVA. (The last few were of course used only for competitions.) On Friday nights, which was mostly all teens, the sign would display ALL SKATE most of the time, but every half hour or so, the COUPLES ONLY would light up, which was the signal for me and my buddies, who weren't yet at the stage where we had coupled off, to skate off the rink and sit down on the hard plastic benches. The older teens would pair up, with the more serious, competition and skate-club skaters circling in their own smaller ring in the middle of the rink, where they showed off their moves while the love birds circled. For the weekend skaters and the seventh graders, we'd mostly use the time as an opportunity to get a slice of pizza or play pinball. There were a few adventurous eighth-grade boys who would ask girls to skate with them.

My friends and I used to talk about doing this, even dare each other, but we never acted on it. We'd use the COUPLES ONLY time to do the more accepted form of flirting—hovering near the girls and behaving in an obnoxious fashion.

At that age the boys were beginning to experiment with

rudimentary, entry-level flirting by turning their teasing energies, usually reserved for each other, onto the girls. One of the pranks that boys always pulled on each other was to push a kid's face into the water bubbler when they were taking a drink, so they'd get water up their nose. Kathy Doucette was a tough girl, generally considered "one of the guys," and at Roll-Land one night John Plath tried it on her. But he pushed her face right into the spigot cover and suddenly her lip was split open and blood was all over the floor. So much for entry-level flirting. Plath, ever the gentleman, gave her the Molly Hatchett T-shirt he had on under his flannel shirt, and she held it to her face until the bleeding stopped. After that incident, among my peers at least, the water bubbler gag was pretty much retired. What a dumb gag that was anyway.

Boys were so obnoxious in their attempt to "impress" the girls. They'd walk up to them and unzip their hoodies, or pull the hood over their head and yank it down over their eyes. The girls would laugh it off and try to be a good sport, but you could see it in their faces—they were barely tolerating the borderline harassment. But it was either that or stay home on a Friday night, which many girls did, and they were probably happier for it. I'm sure I engaged in my share of obnoxious behavior as well, but I also wanted to do things the right way. Roll-Land had this whole system set up and I wanted to take advantage of it. I mean, there was a huge sign on the wall that said COUPLES ONLY that was just waiting for me to put it to use!

Eventually, I got up the nerve to ask a girl to skate with me. It had taken me almost a year of Friday nights, but I had found my moment. She was a dark-haired beauty who I had never seen at Roll-Land before. I was admiring her as my friends and

I passed her in the rink. Then the COUPLES ONLY light appeared, and I knew I had to act. We skated to the benches, and her group was positioned right next to ours.

"You want to skate with me?" I asked her.

"I will, but you have to skate with my friend first," she said, pointing to an overweight, lonely looking girl on the end of the bench. "No one ever pays attention to her."

"OK," I said. It seemed like a pretty good bargain. We skated down to her friend.

"Julie, he wants to ask you something," she said to the chubby girl. Then she turned to me and said, "What's your name?"

"Tom. Yeah, hi. You want to skate?" I asked Julie.

"OK," Julie said.

I took her hand and we went out on the rink. It was the least crowded skating I'd ever done—there was only a handful of couples skating. It was an entirely new experience for me. Sure enough the organist started playing "Somewhere My Love" (Lara's theme from *Doctor Zhivago*), one of his romantic COUPLES ONLY favorites. As we came around the first time, my friends Heyn and Mitiguy were leaning over the railing hooting and hollering.

"A-ROUND and a-ROUND!" Mitiguy yelled at me as I skated by. He was making a fat joke. The girl could surely hear them. I felt bad for her and annoyed with Mitiguy for being such a jerk.

"Don't worry about those guys," I said.

"It's all right."

Something gave me the impression that Julie was used to guys like Mitiguy.

We went around the rink together several times, with Mitiguy yelling out some stupid, mean phrase each time we passed, things like "Fat chance!" and "a-ROUND the world in eighty days!" While I knew the guys were teasing me as well as Julie, I wasn't going to feel embarrassed for myself. I was out there doing a COUPLES ONLY skate, and they weren't.

I said to Julie, "I'm gonna skate with your friend, too. All right?"

"OK."

We skated off and I let go of her hand and rolled alongside the original dark-haired girl.

"Thank you," she said.

"What's your name?" I asked.

"Noel."

"Like No-elle?"

"Yeah, like Christmas."

"I never heard that as a name before. You want to skate?" I asked.

Just then, the ALL SKATE sign lit up.

"Whoops. Maybe next time," said Noel, and off she went skating onto the floor. I'd missed my chance.

But I had held up my end of the bargain, so I waited for the next time COUPLES ONLY flashed on the sign and I looked for Noel, who seemed to be avoiding me. I found her lingering near the pizza window with her friend.

"Can we do that skate now?" I asked her.

"OK." I waited until we got to the entrance and then took her hand. I was actually relieved that I had had the warmup with her friend, so I wasn't self-conscious. I was getting pretty good at COUPLES ONLY.

Nevertheless, when we came around, there again were Mitiguy and Heyn still hooting and hollering. This time the organist was playing "In the Good Old Summer Time," but my buddies were singing "Rock-a-bye Baby . . . !" and making a cradle-rocking gesture with their hands. I didn't get it. When I came around again, they were still at it. "When the bough breaks, the cradle will fall!"

When the ALL SKATE came back on, I let go of her hand and we skated off the rink.

"They're in sixth grade!" yelled Mitiguy when I rolled up. He and Heynzy had spoken to Julie and asked what school she and Noel went to. Turns out, they were sixth graders at St. Catherine's. That's why we'd never seen them before. I had thought they must be from a different town, but it turns out, they were still in elementary school. And the guys were trying to make me feel bad about it. What were the rules for this kind of thing? Lots of guys dated younger girls, right? And I wasn't even dating; I was skating. And those guys should have been cheering, not jeering. Nevertheless, it would take me a while to work up the nerve to ask another girl to COUPLES ONLY skate with me again.

The skating rink became the epicenter of our social life during those early teen years, as we moved our focus from go-carts and baseball to raven-haired girls and, well, for me, more raven-haired girls. In eighth and ninth grade, we moved on to Saturday-night gatherings at Papa Gino's, with girls at one table and boys at another, boys being loud and trying to be noticed, and the girls playing coy and being stingy with their attention. Occasionally one of us would stop by to see what the girls were playing on their mini-jukebox. Gradually, we boys stopped being obnoxious and started being nice, and we found it worked. I see middle school kids out at the mall now, and not much has changed. As radically different

as my early childhood was from the kids' of today, I think
there is something universal about the early-teen years. Even
with Snapchat and instant messaging, and teens being more
sophisticated than ever, there is still no substitute for these
kinds of coed hangouts where kids awkwardly test the waters with each other. Of course, they probably don't do a lot
of roller-skating to Perry Como songs, but the other stuff is
pretty much the same.

CHAPTER 15

BE OPEN-MINDED

MY PARENTS WERE DEVOUT CATHOLICS, BUT MY SIB-
lings and I all went to public school. Tuition was
the deciding factor for many large families, as it
surely was in our budget-conscious home—the idea of paying
property taxes to fund public schools and not making use of
them would have kept my folks awake at night. Another major
factor for Mr. and Mrs. Shillue was that they didn't trust the
Catholic schools of the 1970s to hold firm to the doctrine of
pre–Vatican II Church that they held dear. My mother would
rather I get that important doctrine directly from her. Those
modern schools would never deliver the right and true Cathol-
icism. All the Catholic kids in Norwood public schools (that
is, 90 percent of the school) had to go to CCD* after school

---

* CCD is the Confraternity of Catholic Doctrine, which is known as
 "Sunday school" to many. But there were so many Catholic kids in

one day a week, but most of my religious education came from car rides with my mother, where she would explain the mysteries of our faith, the miracles of the saints, and the power of the Holy Rosary. I would come home from CCD and have my lessons retaught by her. I can remember one lesson in particular that set my mother off. The assignment was to "circle all examples you see of people committing a sin" on a workbook page that featured pictures of various people, some doing obvious good deeds and some obviously sinning. One illustration, however, featured a kid sitting under a tree doing nothing but, apparently, daydreaming. When we reviewed our work at the end of class, the nun pointed out the one we had all apparently gotten wrong: the child who was doing nothing was clearly "sinning" because he was doing nothing. His was a sin of omission: wasting time is a sin when you could be helping others. This then led to discussion about various ways that we could help others in our community, instead of daydreaming. I found the discussion interesting enough that I mentioned it to my mother after I got home. Her emphatic response surprised me: "That lesson is wrong, and sitting around doing nothing is absolutely NOT a sin."

Really? I showed her my book.

"How do we *know* what he is doing?" she asked me as we looked at my workbook together. "He may be thinking of a cure for a disease. He may be about to discover something as important as gravity, like Sir Isaac Newton . . . but even if he isn't, who are we to say what he is doing is a sin? He may be

---

Norwood that the churches couldn't handle teaching them on a busy Sunday, so they bussed all the school kids to the local parish every Wednesday afternoon for classes.

reflecting on the Holy Spirit! Or he may be doing nothing at all. Regardless, daydreaming is not a sin and to call it such is to diminish the whole idea of sin."

When my dad got home from work, my mother showed him the workbook and explained to him the lesson to which I had been subjected. My dad looked it over and then looked at me.

"That . . ." he said, "is a load of bunk."

Dad's lessons were always more condensed than Mom's, but I knew they were both on the same page about things like this. I probably wouldn't have given much thought to this workbook lesson, but their decisive take on the issue and their unequivocal rejection of it stuck with me. Not the lesson itself, but the clarity with which they approached their beliefs. They didn't just go to church on Sunday; they liked to think about the doctrine and discuss it, and if they read or heard something they disagreed with, they'd challenge it. In this way, they were very devout but they were also rebels—they were ready to challenge anyone in the church, whether a nun, a priest, a bishop, or a pope, if they disagreed with them. While they never questioned their faith, they were more than willing to question the hierarchy of the Church if it went against their beliefs. So as a kid, the Church to me was mostly about doing what you were told and following the Ten Commandments, but as I got older it became more about understanding the ideas behind faith, and my parents encouraged that.

My mother would take me to church in these early adolescent years but she'd let me wander off. Teens liked to gather in the back. At the crowded Masses people young and old would stand in the back vestibule and peer through the stained-glass windows. As a little kid I always thought the people in the back were a little guilty of something, like they didn't want to go all the way into the church because they had done something wrong that week. In some instances that may have been true. I thought I'd never be a back-of-the-church person.

But as a teen, some of the other kids would gather in the back—then sneak up the staircase leading to the organ loft. The curved staircase had a triangular landing halfway up that functioned as a sort of meeting place for teenagers. We'd sit and talk the whole time but were still able to feel like we attended Mass. We'd barely hear the priest but we could hear the choir and feel the pipe organ as it vibrated the carpeted staircase under us. I'd look forward to these Masses because we had our own private space to talk, which is all we wanted to do in those days, talk with other people our own age.

Later on, in high school, my friends and I would skip Mass altogether and just meet at the Apollo Restaurant, which shared its parking lot with St. Catherine's parish. We'd spend our "Mass" time eating eggs and drinking coffee and getting philosophical. We called it the Apolostic Church and justified our skipping church by allowing only theological or philosophical discussion at the table. The Apolostic Church was for discussion of deep thoughts—it wasn't merely to justify our transgressions; we were on a spiritual quest. We'd bring our dog-eared copies of New Age bestsellers by Richard Bach and Robert Pirsig to our church breakfast and discuss great ideas. Jacked up on caffeine and metaphysics, one discussion would flow into the next without pause. We were so impressed with ourselves and our expanding minds, we thought we were the only teens to ever do such a thing. No one bothered to tell us "thinking you're the smartest person that ever lived" is a phase every adolescent goes through.

But my routine was still the same: I'd arrive at St. Catherine's with my mother, and when she walked inside the church, I'd just turn around, walk down the stairs, and head over to the Apolostic for breakfast and heresy with my friends. Then I'd meet her outside the church after Mass thinking she was the most naïve person in the world. More likely she was using the same technique that she used when I was using stolen money to gorge on candy at Dacey's variety store in the first grade—laissez faire parenting. She knew I was skipping church! But what good would it be to drag me into the pews at that age when I'd already been to Mass more than eight hundred times, and had countless theological discussions with her in the car. At that point, it had either sunk in or it hadn't. If it had, she knew I'd eventually find my way back.

Well, guess what, her master plan worked. My wife and I take the kids to church faithfully every Sunday morning. Chalk another one up for their parenting style. How many is that now?

*

Despite what I thought when I was in grade school, there weren't just Catholics in Norwood; there were families of other religions, too. Those families mostly lived far away from the area where we lived, though, as our little corner was most definitely the Irish Catholic part of town. This meant that I wasn't really exposed to anybody who wasn't Irish Catholic until junior high school, when students from all different grammar schools came together. Now we had Greeks, Protestants, Jews, Catholics, and *one* black kid. It was like the United Nations!

I was immediately attracted to the Jewish girls. They were mysterious to me. I remember looking over at their lunch table that first day in junior high. There wasn't a Jewish table—we weren't ethnically separated or anything, but a group of them all sat together. The first thing I noticed was their dark hair, my weakness. And they also dressed well, and knew how to wear makeup. Junior high, at least in those days, was when girls first started experimenting with makeup, and let's just say the Irish Catholic girls weren't so skilled in that department. They kind of slapped it on. It looked as if they applied it hastily on the way to school, while they were trying to hold on to a little mirror and smoke a cigarette with the other hand. (OK, not many of the girls in junior high smoked but I'm trying to paint a picture—some of those Irish girls were tough.) The Jewish girls seemed to know how to wear their makeup tastefully—they were able to blend their foundation down through the neck area, so they didn't have that harsh makeup line at the jaw. Irish Catholic girls just stopped at the edge of the face, and said, "I'm done . . . whatevah!"

And around the eyes, Jewish girls were of course very subtle—maybe just a touch of mascara. Those Irish girls would draw a black line around the eye. A nice, thick black line inside the eyelashes. It made them look like they'd been in a fight or wanted to fight me.

I'm drawing a bit of a contrast here, because that's what my young mind was drawing. I was attracted to something different. This was a new era, and I wanted to branch out.

I remember one day in junior high, sitting at the lunch table, looking over at those Jewish girls. I told my friend Mitiguy that I liked the way the Jewish girls looked, and he just shook his head slowly as he drank his carton of milk. "Don't even bother," he said, with the straw sticking out of the side of his mouth. "They only date other Jews."

Well, I was certainly up for making gross generalizations about an entire people, but Mitiguy took it to extremes. I'll never forget him sucking on his milk telling me I couldn't date Jewish girls. Where did he get his information? He was pretty savvy on matters such as this. His parents were divorced and the single-parent kids always had access to information nobody else had. I guess it's because parents spend a lot of energy trying to keep their kids from learning about certain things, and if there's only one of them instead of two, a lot of that stuff is bound to slip through—kind of like a power play in hockey. So Mitiguy was always the most "worldly" among us.

And he says I can't date Jewish girls? Bring it on, I thought. I was in eighth grade and there wasn't a tradition I wasn't willing to tackle head-on. I was ready to stretch the confines of my Catholic youth at that point. It wasn't a religious thing as much as cultural. I wanted to get out of my comfort zone.

So, I went after the Jewish girls. I went right up to that lunch table and tried out my dad's #1 move: I smiled at 'em. And they kind of liked me. Or at least they appreciated that I liked them. And that's all I was looking for. At this stage, there wasn't any real "dating" anyway. The basic routine was: you'd hang around them in the lunch room, then find out if they were going to be at the library after school so you could accidentally run into them, then one day maybe follow them home without their permission, then sit on their porch and have an uncomfortable conversation. I know these days that's called "stalking" but this was a more innocent time.

But the important thing was, I was stretching my horizons, unafraid to venture beyond my comfort zone. I would not be restrained by the Mitiguys of the world—there were new lands to explore, and like Magellan I was ready to discover the unknown.

CHAPTER 16

BE(AT) IT

I WENT HAPPILY ALONG IN MY 1950S-LIKE CHILDHOOD, right up to the dawn of the 1980s, quite literally actually. John Mitiguy and I took the train into Boston for the "First Night" celebration on December 31, 1979. We walked through the streets at Downtown Crossing, past the Old Statehouse and the sight of the Boston Massacre, surrounded by jugglers, stilt-walkers, mimes, ice sculptures, and street musicians. I'd been there so many times before with my dad, but this was the first time I'd been in the city on my own. As kids he would take us not just to the Freedom Trail but also to the Museum of Science and sailing at the Community Boating dock on the Charles River. If we came in on a Sunday, my dad would take us to church downtown. One time after Mass we were walking through the downtown area and I asked my father, "Does anyone live here?"

"Yeah, people live here, all right. Half these buildings have apartments in them."

"I could never live here," I said.

"Oh, you say that now, but in ten years you're not going to want to live anywhere else."

My dad was usually pretty smart, but I remember thinking this seemed way off base. I couldn't imagine I would ever want to live in the city. It was so noisy and you couldn't see the sun. I loved the suburbs with its trees and grass and ball fields and pools. But walking around Boston with my friend that New Year's Eve, I started to get a glimpse of it—I could picture myself living in the city as a young man. Maybe my dad had been right.

Down a side street along Fanueil Hall there was someone performing on a small stage beneath a banner that read "One Man Band"; to my surprise, he was not a man with a big bass drum contraption with symbols, hi-hats, and xylophones attached to it playing Bavarian-style oompah music as you'd imagine when you hear the phrase "one-man band," but a lone performer standing behind a stack of synthesizers. He had a pale face and wore thick black eyeliner like an Irish Catholic schoolgirl, and he was playing a song that sounded like nothing I'd ever heard before. It was, indeed, the music of an entire band coming from one man. The pulsing, bass-heavy electronic music was accompanied by a drum machine and sounded like outer space music to me. More than in my ears, I could feel the sound in my chest as it vibrated my lungs. The wan, androgynous man was surrounded by laser lights as he played, and I found the performance totally off-putting yet strangely exciting. I stood with other gawkers and watched the whole song. I vividly recall the lyrics: "Here in my car, I feel safest of all."

The street musician known as the One Man Band was playing a cover of the song "Cars" by Gary Numan. The song was currently climbing the charts in the UK, but was unknown to U.S. audiences. A few months later, Gary Numan would play the song on *Saturday Night Live* and it would become a top ten hit in the United States, too. I remember feeling that since I'd seen the song performed before everyone else in the suburbs, I was ahead of the crowd, and on the cutting edge.

In Boston that New Year's Eve, I imagined that the car that the One Man Band was singing about was some futuristic bubble car that glided along an elevated highway above the ground into a new decade. Being in the city at night, with the music, and the lights, and fireworks, I already felt like I was in a dream. I felt a little stoned even though all I'd had was ginger ale and caramel popcorn. I was thinking, *This is it. I'm almost grown up, it's the future, and I'm here to see it arrive.*

Most people don't get to realize they are part of an era until it has passed. No one knew the Great Depression would come upon them suddenly on Black Tuesday in 1929. Similarly, people didn't wake up in the 1950s with the idea that they were living in Happy Days. But as I stood there taking in the weirdness of this performance, it seemed like the '80s was being given a ribbon-cutting ceremony right there for me that night. I had grown up in small-town America, and I loved it. But I was ready to take on this new world in this new decade. I didn't have the nostalgia for my childhood that I have now, so I was more than willing to leave it behind. That prospect was exciting but also a little scary, only not in the way that I was used to. As I have said, I spent a lot of my childhood in fear, but it was fear in the context of a world that was small, contained, and safe. Whatever the future was about to bring, it seemed, like the eerie street performer with the synthesizers, both thrilling and slightly disquieting.

CHAPTER 17

BE ROGUE

I N THE SPRING OF MY SOPHOMORE YEAR OF HIGH school I bought an unlined, blank, hardcover book so I could begin keeping a diary, although I called it a journal because I found the word *diary* vaguely feminine. I even wrote "Tom Shillue—A Journal" on the inside cover to make it absolutely clear. In any case I wanted to get my thoughts and feelings down on paper.

When I read my diary now, I see that it is the story of a young man trying his *hardest* to be angry and complicated. I don't think I was really very angry, and I don't think I had any reason to be, but I sure wanted to be. I remember putting the words to the paper with the purpose of shocking my future self with my rebelliousness.

This is an excerpt from my diary:

> *Today, I'm being dragged off to a wake with my family. I hate*
> *wakes, and there is no reason for me to go except for the fact that*
> *my father wants to show everyone that his son has respect for the*
> *dead. By the way, the deceased is Aunt Norah. I don't even know*
> *her last name, or know what she looks like. They'll be relatives who*
> *are coming from all around just to see her who don't know what*
> *she looks like either. It's funny how people don't bother coming to*
> *visit you until you're already in a pine box. Nobody likes wakes.*
> *Everybody just goes to them because everybody else is going to*
> *be there. Habits like that start early in life. In high school, half*
> *the kids at the football games hate football. Most everybody else*
> *couldn't care less. And at the weekend parties, "aren't you going?*
> *Everybody else is going to be there." I could talk about the wrongs*
> *of high school parties forever, but I'll save that for another time.*

But perhaps what I should find more embarrassing than my misplaced, overblown anger is the fact that the early pages of "Tom Shillue—A Journal" have to do exclusively with my chief passion of the time, Dungeons and Dragons.

I was running with a new crowd—I never really broke with Heyn and Mitiguy, but as we entered high school we slowly began to go our separate ways. My new friend Bob, who I'd met through our "Apolostic Church" of Sunday-morning philosophy, and I wanted to play D&D, shorthand for Dungeons and Dragons for you non-nerds. We had heard of this mysterious game through word of mouth but we didn't know where to go to learn about it, because it was the 1980s and there were no Facebook pages or Reddit groups to consult; you had to learn things from actual people. But, one name came to mind: Rob Morrissey. He used to sit all by himself at the Apollo restaurant with his sketchpad. He was an artist, a loner, and a brooding cynic who read comic books. He was surely into that kind of thing.

Bob and I approached Rob in the art room and asked him.

"I don't know," he said. "I know what you're talking about, but I don't know how to do it. I'm not a dungeon master."

"What's a dungeon master?"

"You need a dungeon master to play. They know how everything is done with that game. I think I might know somebody, though—Greg Heckmann. He's in my social studies class. He's a little weird, but I'm sure he knows what he's doing."

"Can you talk to him?"

"I know where his locker is."

So, Bob, Rob, and I walked up to Greg's locker between classes. We found him just standing there, staring into his open locker. He was about six feet tall and very pale with blond hair. It seemed like he knew we were there, but didn't turn to acknowledge us when we got up next to him.

"We heard you might be a dungeon master," I said, nervously. This guy radiated creepy.

He kept staring straight ahead into his locker. "I might be," he said.

"Do you think we could get you to . . . referee for us?"

"You mean D.M.?" He turned his head and stared at me blankly, like Christopher Walken in *The Deer Hunter*. "You need to create characters first. You have to be serious. Are you guys serious about this?"

All three of us nodded. "Yes. We're very serious."

Greg looked around at all three of us, summing us up. Then he looked beyond us, as if to make sure no one else was listening. "Be at my house at ten in the morning on Saturday," he said, slamming his locker shut. As he brushed past us and headed down the hallway, he added, "I'm the white house at the end of Bond Street. Come to the back and knock on the basement door."

This guy was the weirdest kid in the school.

Just what we were looking for.

On the next Saturday we knocked on the door and watched it open with a creak. He walked away without a greeting and we followed. The unfinished basement had a concrete floor and stone walls, and was lit by the sunlight of the small eye-level windows. Greg sat at the head of a square wooden table surrounded by four chairs. He had a binder, three pads of paper and pencils, and various sets of dice.

"First things first, you've got to roll to create your characters," he said.

We sat at the table and began the painstaking process of creating characters by rolling die after die. After we were done Greg took us through a beginner dungeon. For those unfamiliar with D&D, it's just talking. The dungeon master describes the action and asks questions, and the players answer. There is no game board or figurines. The entire game takes place in the imagination. We played all day, pausing only long enough for a run to Nick's for veal Parmesan subs, which we took back to Greg's house to eat while we continued playing. When we finally stumbled out of the basement it was dark, and we walked home in a daze. Like most D&D players, we were hooked after the first hit.

I'm not sure how my friends and I spent all our free time before that day, but after that, all our weekends were booked. D&D was exactly what we needed. You see, we were beyond Roll-Land and Papa Gino's, where boys and girls would congregate in groups and horse around on a Friday night. We were in high school now and people were dating. But not us, not yet.

There is something about a boy's mind at that age; I think that the body is aware that it is about to be overtaken by a complete obsession with women that far exceeds your early teen years. The body knows it's powerful, and will soon become all consuming, so the mind tries to distract itself as long as it can with activities like D&D. The maps, the hit-points, the treasure, the details. It's why teenaged boys of the 1970s loved *The Lord of the Rings*. It's full of maps and family trees, all perfect for memorizing: "Aragorn, Son of Arathorn! Gimli, Son of Gloin!" The more details, the better. You're trying to fill your mind with stuff to take up space and keep it busy before the total onslaught of women. The final battle. The end of boyhood. The point of no return.

We'd play from Friday afternoon to Sunday night, with a short break at the Apolostic Church on Sunday at 11 a.m. My parents weren't thrilled with my D&D addiction, but they put up with it and chalked it up to my being "creative." They were also surprisingly tolerant of its occult themes. My mother took it in stride, occasionally correcting me if I was excitedly talking about one of our adventures.

"How was your game?" she'd ask.

"Amazing. We killed a Beholder and captured a gnome god. . . ."

"That's nice but there's only one God," she'd remind me.

*

When you look at my journal from high school you can divide it into two distinct sections: before girls and after. The first part of the diary references only two things: Dungeons, and Dragons. To wit:

> *Yesterday Greg, Rob, Bob and myself established the Dungeons & Dragons Hall of Fame. So far the members are Corbon the Great, Crimp Kadiva, Nuklo Vadantus, and Gorian the Brave. This weekend is all Dungeons & Dragons. We'll start Friday night. It will be one of the best adventures ever.*

Then the next entry:

> *Yesterday's Dungeons & Dragons adventure was the best ever! I was the unsung hero. I helped kill the Frost Giant Chief and did excellent throughout the entire adventure. The dance this weekend was cancelled because of snow but we'll play some pretty good D&D.*

Are you seeing a pattern here?

> *Our characters teleported from the glacial rift of the Frost Giant Garl to five miles north to the Five Fire Giant settlement. Now they're nice and warm.*
>
> *Fire Giants are bigger and meaner than Frost Giants. We played Dungeons and Dragons again tonight. It was pretty good. We killed a few Fire Giants and then just walked through the place taking all the treasure. I have the entire adventure in the Dungeons and Dragons log.**

---

* Yes, apparently in addition to my diary there was a Dungeons and Dragons log, which has, alas, been lost to history. I'm sure its pages were filled with more detail about Fire Giants than anyone has ever wanted to know.

If you are a healthy teenage young man and you are writing entries like that in your journal, then some self-reflection and redirection of priorities might be in order. We'd been playing *every* weekend during the school year, so when summer arrived, in an attempt to save ourselves from losing all of the pigment in our skin and turning into social outcasts forever, Bob and I tried out for a summer play—a rootin' tootin' wild-west musical. We claimed our newfound interest in theater was an intellectual pursuit, something to pass the time between dungeons, but I'm pretty sure it wasn't the mind at work but the body, and we were drawn to the theater for the same reason most guys are: the female-to-male ratio is always in our favor.

I immediately fell for one of the actresses, Anne Lynch. She was playing the lead role, the delicate ingénue Rose Blossom, and I was the wisecracking cowboy sidekick Wild Bill Hickock. I was sure she would go for Bob, ever the handsome leading man, but that was not the case. I heard through the hooker-with-a-heart-of-gold Calamity Jane that the beautiful Rose Blossom had an eye for ol' Wild Bill. Which was fine with Bob because he had a thing for Anne's sister Sharon.

Bob and I would go out with the sisters after rehearsal, just to hang around and talk or to go get an ice cream. Then one night, the girls showed up in their parents' car, a big Chevy Impala. We drove to the junior high school parking lot and parked next to the tennis courts. Bob and Sharon went for a walk, leaving Anne and me alone in the car.

I put an Elvis Costello cassette in the player and Anne turned and reclined against her door. The Impala was as big as a living room. I tried to subtly inch across the front seat toward Anne. The lights were shining through the fence of the tennis courts, casting a diamond chain-link shadow across her, following the contours of her face and neck and continuing down over her tank top and shorts. I drank it in as I inched toward her. The yellow light on her tanned skin and the diamond shadow that draped over her is burned in my memory forever. It's my own personal Edward Hopper painting, "Young Woman Lit Through Fence."

It took me 14 minutes and 39 seconds to get my arms around her. I know that because "Man Out of Time" is the fifth track on Elvis Costello's *Imperial Bedroom*, and the song started just as I touched her. By the time I kissed her, Elvis Costello was singing the chorus.

I kissed Anne Lynch for the rest of the summer. I only stopped to eat and sleep and do the necessary things required for living during the daytime. Bob did the same with Sharon. It was the legendary summer of the Lynch Sisters. And it took a swinging broadsword to our D&D game. Greg and Rob weren't too happy about this development. They continued playing without us, rolling for our characters, who *coincidentally* came to an untimely end in the Temple of Elemental Evil. They claimed it was all in the dice. I'd kiss Anne until my lips were sore, but if you look in my journal/diary, you see . . . nothing. I didn't write one word about it. The feelings were so intense that I was not prepared to write about them. Here is the first entry after months of not writing, just as my whirlwind summer romance was coming to an end:

> *I have not written in this book for many months. I look back at what I wrote before, I get sick to my stomach. This book is supposed to record my personal thoughts and feelings, and I'm*

*writing a summary of Dungeons. It does not even seem like me
who wrote all that Dungeons and Dragons crap.*

*How moronic. Any thoughts which I tried to put into words
were destroyed by my inability to express myself properly. I must
make note of this so that when I'm an adult and I read this, I
don't get the impression I was completely illiterate as a child. I am
going over to Anne Lynch's house tomorrow. She's got to talk to
me about stuff that's too difficult to write about. I'll be right glad
to see her, because I didn't see her at all on the weekend. I haven't
played Dungeons and Dragons since the play began. I kind of lost
interest because we got so powerful.*

As is typical in my diary, I display a great lack of insight
into my feelings. I write that I lost interest in Dungeons and
Dragons because our "characters got so powerful." The direct
correlation between my relationship with Anne and the end of
my interest in role-playing games goes completely unnoticed.
(Also, note the part where I mention Anne having to talk about
stuff that's "too difficult to write about" while glossing over
what was obviously our impending breakup.)

But the seed had been planted. I couldn't go back to Dungeons and Dragons. I cast the die aside, never to be rolled again.
Body and mind were united in my devotion to the pursuit of
women.

CHAPTER 18

BE NEW WAVE

I'T'S NO WONDER THAT SO MANY YOUNG MEN ARE PRONE to fantasize about women instead of taking action. Our preteen obsessions were all based in fantasy. For my generation it was *The Six Million Dollar Man*, *Star Wars*, Marvel comics, Dungeons and Dragons. Today it is Minecraft, still *Star Wars*, still Marvel comics . . . why should we all of a sudden be particularly adept at dealing with girls the minute our voices change? It's not as if we were ever actually flying the Millennium Falcon, or really sacking castles and making off with treasure; we were only pretending to do those things. Then, when it comes to women, we are expected to jump right in and behave realistically with them, these strange creatures, as puzzling to us as a gelatinous cube is to a level-one thief with a three-hit-point dagger.

Besides, we didn't know anything! And there was no way to learn except through experience. We didn't have the Internet to turn to for any wonderful or terrible thing we might be curious about. Today, of course, the average American kid can be transported from the privacy of home to the equivalent of the red light district in seconds via his high-speed modem. But what did we have? An old hollowed-out tree in the woods, inside which could be found a handful of rolled-up *Playboy* magazines. Ask any suburban kid who grew up in the '70s or '80s, and they can tell you where the tree that contained the magazines was located. But all that offered was a few glimpses of something mysterious. It didn't have the power to offer an alternative to the safe and ordered world we grew up in. And part of that safe, ordered world was: no sex.

It wasn't allowed. Good girls didn't do it, and good guys didn't try to make them. So I went through those high school years with no expectation of it—and I'm so glad that I did. I really think the key to happiness at that age is not having sex. It's also important that *there is hope or expectation* that you'll be having any. Adolescents have enough to struggle with; they don't need to add that to the equation. And it's not about being "safe" or any of that modern stuff. It really comes down to the good old-fashioned advice: that sex is best left until marriage, and if you're not going to wait until you're married, you had better at least wait until you're an adult. And the longer you delay it, the better.

Now, I would give this advice to any young person today, and mostly for entirely secular reasons, because I think it's a better way to get through those teen years and remain happy.

But of course it all comes from religious morality. That's what holds it all together. You're not going to get anywhere with a teenage boy by saying, "Believe me, you'll be happier without it." You may sincerely believe it and have the life experience to back it up, but he'll just smile at you and say, "I'll take my chances." You've got to instill it early on, and that's where the religious stuff comes in.

I hear my contemporaries complain about how they "grew up with a lot of Catholic guilt." What's the matter with that? Guilt is fantastic. I thrived on it in high school, and it was responsible for keeping me in line. It wasn't able to keep me from having impure thoughts, but it kept me from wallowing in them. It didn't stop me from lusting after girls, but it kept me from pressuring them to do anything beyond making out—which I loved to do, because it was as far as I ever expected to get. And expectations, as I said, are extremely important—instead of spending my high school years feeling like I was stranded on first base, every time I kissed a girl I felt like I was hitting the home run derby.

So even though I was not focused on having sex, I was very focused on the opposite sex.

I was determined not to go back to rolling twenty-sided die, and I wasn't going to be intimidated. I had landed Anne Lynch, after all, and even though she had unceremoniously dumped me at the end of the summer, for a time my charm and sense of humor had won her over. I needed to be proactive and put myself out there. I put my dad's lesson to work all through high school. I'd smile at 'em in the hallways, smile at 'em in class or in the stands at the football games. I was always polite, as I had been taught. Some guys teased girls; I simply smiled at 'em. The jocks were busy trying to look cool, and the nerds were too intimidated to ever look cool; and there I was, with eye contact, a confident smile, and a "how-do-you-do?" It certainly wasn't cool—the ladies weren't really sure what to make of me, but they liked me. Maybe they didn't have a crush on me and perhaps they didn't understand me, but they always smiled back. I had their attention.

So I was the nice guy, but I wasn't going to be one of those nice guys who finish last. I was also starting to craft my persona as an outsider at this time. An iconoclast. I was "alternative." At least I thought I was. But that's what being alternative is—thinking you are different from everyone else.

To create my alternative persona I borrowed cues from the music I was listening to. I decided I was new wave/post punk. The new wave friends I had recently made were listening to U2, Joe Jackson, the Police, Depeche Mode, the Specials, the Clash, and Elvis Costello. The average suburban New England kid back then referred to all this as "punk" even though it wasn't. MTV was brand new and was sweeping the nation, but hadn't really reached small-town America. Everyone still listened to hard rock like AC/DC and Zeppelin, or southern bands like Lynyrd Skynyrd and Molly Hatchett. Being on the cutting edge of new music, my friends and I became a small crew of weirdos, and it felt good to be outsiders.

I put my outsider status out there in what I chose to wear, as most teenagers do. I had to live up to my alternative persona, but I didn't have enough money to go to Chess King every weekend and buy one of those awesome shirts with all the buttons and flaps that had been knocked off from a Duran Duran album cover, so I would shop at thrift stores.

I mixed and matched my vintage findings and cobbled together a classic/new wave, Bing-Crosby-meets-the-Eurythmics look. Picture Duckie from the movie *Pretty in Pink* if he were . . . Actually, just picture Duckie, because he totally stole my look. It was sufficiently offbeat to keep everyone guessing, including my parents, who nonetheless took it all in stride. This may seem surprising, given the very traditional upbringing I've described, but by high school, my parents gave me a lot of freedom to do what I wanted. Even though I had been literally tied to a tree as a kid, as a teen I was given a fairly long leash to be offbeat and a little weird. So although they may not have agreed with all the ways I was expressing myself, they let it go. Some of it may have been exhaustion, seeing as I was their fourth child to go through adolescence, and later kids always seem to get the benefit of more laid-back parenting. But I think a lot of it was their deliberate philosophy: they had given me the foundation in my childhood, and it was time to trust that it had sunk in, and let me learn things on my own.

My favorite secondhand store was a little gem in South Norwood called the Norwood Women's Community Committee Thrift Shop, which I still maintain might have been the best thrift store in America. After a man's untimely death, a wife would donate his entire wardrobe to the shop. These were men from the greatest generation, too: they had Savile-tailored three-piece suits, Harris Tweed overcoats, Stetson fedora hats, leather wingtip shoes, and white bucks. Everything sold for five to ten dollars. I bought as much as I could afford. I guess it's no surprise for someone who had such an old-school child-hood, but as I was trying to push the envelope and be edgy and modern, I ended up going full retro. I guess I was still clinging to the 1950s, even then.

*

On Saturday nights we'd go to dances at Xaverian Brothers, an all-boys Catholic high school that, improbably, was the hottest social scene in south suburban Massachusetts. Whoever booked the bands for the Xaverian dances had their finger on the pulse of the moment. And those dances had the lure of exclusivity—girls from all over the area were welcome, but only Xaverian boys. Boys who weren't students at Xaverian could only gain entry by way of a special "voucher" signed by an Xaverian student. These vouchers were like gold and traded aggressively on the high school black market. Public school girls were used as both the bait and the prize. All the public high school guys put the word out to all the girls that if an Xaverian boy asked you to their dance, you had to ask for a voucher "for a friend's boyfriend" so that the non-private school guys could get in on the action. The girls didn't seem to mind being used that way—the more guys there, the more competition over them. All of the extra work required to simply get through the door just made the whole event more desirable, even though these dances were just a bunch of high school kids packed into a humid gymnasium.

My friends and I didn't go to the dances to hit on girls and try to get them to make out with us behind the bleachers; that's what the Xaverian guys and the jocks from our school did. We showed up in our skinny ties ready to dance. We'd be out on the floor the whole night, working up such a sweat on that steamy dance floor that we would soak through our extremely carefully chosen outfits. Then, at the stroke of 11 p.m., the lights would go up, and we had to step out sopping wet into the freezing cold and walk home.

Sometimes Dicky Barrett would show up to the Xaverian dances and bring his Boston swagger with him. Dicky was still a student at Norwood High, but he spent most of his weekend nights in the Boston clubs. He knew the whole punk scene. His older brother was a bit of a local celebrity, the lead singer for the Boston band Chain Link Fence, which was very big at the time. This is how Chuck Warner, who ran the garage-rock label Throbbing Lobster, described Chain Link Fence:

> "Believe it or not these guys started off as an unbelievably earnest and sloppy popthrash band, but Billy had his heart set on being a crooner . . . Billy's younger brother Dicky Barrett couldn't understand why I wouldn't sign his band, too. I told him every rhythm section should know how to play ska, but no one should be allowed to record it. Heh." *

Of course, Dicky would go on to prove him wrong a decade later by hitting it big with his suddenly very mainstream "skacore" band the Mighty Mighty Bosstones. Skacore, a mix of the british ska and hardcore punk, was a genre he basically invented.

---

* Chuck Warner, "Throb Story," *Hyped to Death* (blog), https://www .hyped2death.com/throbstory.html.

But in high school he was still the little brother to Billy, and Dicky liked to show up at Xaverian and expose us rubes to the kind of stuff that was going on in the Boston punk clubs. I remember one winter night the band at the dance was playing a cover of the B-52's *Strobe Light* and Dicky started throwing himself into the crowd of suburban high school boys. The lighting guy in the gym set off the strobe light for about ten seconds, sending all the action on the floor into a sort of stop-motion movie. The strobe light continued to turn on and off, following Dicky around as he slammed into a bunch of guys, who reacted just the way a bunch of high school jocks would when some punk kid runs into them: they retaliated by knocking him into some other kids, who also pushed back. At one point, Dicky got thrown into me and I took a pretty sharp elbow to the chest. Eventually the whole dance floor was pushing one another and it looked like a riot was going to break out. This only encouraged Dicky, and he then started grabbing innocent bystanders and throwing them into the fray. A couple of security guys appeared from nowhere and, as the strobe light turned on, I watched Dicky get dragged, in stop motion, to the side door and thrown out into the freezing cold as he yelled, "Wake up! Don't you fuckin' losers know what slam dancing is!"

That was the kind of attitude I wanted to emulate, but I had to put my own twist on it. Dicky had gone from playground hooligan to punk rocker, but that wasn't me. If Dicky was Sid Vicious of the Sex Pistols, I was more Fred Schneider of the B-52's.

So I became an art room kid in high school. It was the best way to flex my alterna cred. We had a great art program, and all the artsy kids would hang out in that room all day, because this was the only outlet for the weird kids, since there was no theater program. Like most high school art rooms, ours featured a ragtag group of burnouts, weirdoes, hippies, and freaks, along with other countercultural types. I wasn't any of these things, but I was restless and creative and wanted to be *something*. Something beyond the Boy Scout, the altar boy, the normal kid that I'd always been and wanted so desperately to put behind me. I wish I could go back and have a conversation with that kid and tell him not to try so hard. But he probably wouldn't listen, as he would find me to be so very uncool.

But I was on a mission. Bob and I formed a band called Bat Patrol. I was the lead singer, dressed as Batman, with a cape and cowl and black Doc Marten boots. Bob played guitar and dressed as Robin, but with silver shorts and boots like Ziggy Stardust. We did mostly Ramones covers, because the songs were so easy to learn (three chords, man!). As with everything else, this was all done to impress girls. The idea was to be weird, extraordinary, and edgy.

When you craft yourself as *alt*, you can't cast a very wide net when it comes to the ladies. There were basically only three girls who were buying what I was selling, and they were all art room girls. First, there was Jennifer, the Molly Ringwald of Norwood High. She had henna-dyed red hair that was teased out to the max and was always decked out in Cyndi Lauper attire. She walked the hallways in rhythm, like the Go-Go's were constantly playing in her head. She was the living embodiment of the '80s. Then there was Susan. If Jennifer was Molly Ringwald, then Susan was Ally Sheedy. A loner, quiet and cynical, she was an emotional fortress. She rolled her eyes at Jennifer and others like her, and she wouldn't give me the time of day. So, of course, she kept my attention for that reason alone. The last was Catherine. She was very "normal," and didn't even seem like an art room girl on the surface. She was, but she was plain and friendly and never played any games or tried to hide her affection for me. Because she so clearly liked me, I held it against her. She was too normal for me. I wanted Ally Sheedy or Molly Ringwald.

The art room was not for layabouts. The program was run by the serious and charismatic Ms. Jackie Munroe, and she ran it like a conservatory. Students had to produce work; they couldn't just phone it in and expect to pass. There were two daily classes, art and art studio, and for the small group of us who took them both, combined with a study hall which had an open period that we could use as we pleased, we spent three hours a day in the art room. Among the juniors and seniors there were about twenty of us who did this, and we called ourselves "the art majors." My sister had been an art major, and gone on to art school at RISD. My friends Bob, Rob, and Greg were all art majors along with me. But we were all "artists" of different stripes and would use the art room for our own projects. Dicky Barrett basically used it as an extension of his music; he would spend all his time making flyers and drawing cartoons of dancing punks in plaid pants and work boots. He was obsessed with plaid. He'd cover pieces of scrap paper with an intricate tartan patterns and leave them taped to the walls around school. The swatch of plaid meant "Dicky was here." Others, like my friend Grover, were fine artists. He wanted to open a studio by the sea, paint landscapes, and sell them in the galleries on Cape Cod. I did silkscreening and charcoal drawing, and photography, but I didn't really have "my thing" yet.

Ms. Jackie invited an artist-in-residence to Norwood High to expose us to a professional. Fine art painter Harry always smelled like turpentine, was covered in paint speckles, and constantly dished out cynical advice. He drove an old beat-up Saab, and on the weekends, a group of us would pile into his car and drive to his studio in the Fort Point Channel warehouse district along Boston Harbor. The building was in a rough neighborhood and was filled with artists and craftsmen of all types. This was the real art world. It seemed so exciting, and even though he was always warning us about the economic risks of choosing art as a career, I remember thinking that this would be a great way to live. Who needs a lot of money when you can spend your life in a big, spacious building and do whatever kind of work you want?

His studio was filled with rack after rack of his huge paintings. They all had a similar look—incomprehensibly dark and abstract imagery made with very thick paint. They made absolutely no sense to me, but seemed cool. I remember one of his paintings vividly: black and green lines twisting upward and bursting into more darkness. It was titled *The Forest Primeval*. It seemed profound even though I wasn't sure what *primeval* meant. Some of the paintings, which had been given gallery spots, had prices attached to the back wooden frame of the canvas—$800, $900, $1,200. I couldn't believe those figures. He seemed to have a fortune's worth of paintings stored in this loft that was locked with only a padlock. I wanted to know how much money he made on this artwork, but I didn't want to ask in front of the others. When he was out in the hallway having a cigarette by the fire escape, I sneaked out to ask.

"Harry, how often do you sell one of them?"

"What? My paintings? Oh, I've never sold one."

He said it offhandedly, as if he never expected to sell one. I couldn't believe it. He's a full-time painter and he sells nothing? Even my mother sold some of her work, and her studio was in our dining room. If I was going to be an artist, I would have to be able to sell my work. I wouldn't enjoy it otherwise. What good is doing work that nobody wants?

One day Harry announced he had a special trip planned. "This one's for you, Tom," he said.

Harry had taken an interest in me because I was always using my time in the art room to put on "shows." I liked to explain what my work meant more than I liked creating it. Every critique session was an opportunity for me to get some laughs and perform a running monologue about life. I guess he figured I was more of a performer than an artist. When he asked if I had aspirations in that field, I answered, "I haven't really thought about it." But of course I had.

He took us on foot from his studio through the cobble-stone streets of Boston to some other old, dilapidated building in the neighborhood. We took a freight elevator up to a loft space that was crowded with fabric and 3-D sculptures. We sat on the floor and the show began. Lights, music, and two young women "puppeteers" appeared who brought fabric sculptures to life. They sprung up from the floor and danced to the music. They looked like animals, or industrial machines, or insects. The show was avant-garde, or as Grover said, "wicked weahd." It was art and performance together, and it opened up a world of possibilities in my mind.

I was always thinking about what I wanted to be at that time, whether I was going to be an artist or a musician. But that day I realized that maybe I could mix them together in some way, and do my own thing. I could forge my own path, even though I had no idea what that path was going to be.

CHAPTER 19

BE SUPPORTIVE

I BEGAN MY SENIOR YEAR OF HIGH SCHOOL WITH AN AP-propriate amount of rebellious energy. Is there a single diary written by a kid that age that doesn't include an entry in this vein?

August 17—Just because I came in late last night, my dad says "No more late nights. You're not going to be out of this house again after midnight." What a goon. All he had to say was "Don't do it" and I wouldn't do it. Instead he plays the fucking warden and lays down the law. My mother knew exactly what she was doing. She told me how scared she was all night, right in front of him, which would surely convince Dad to take over. He's got no problem trying to control situations such as this. He just does what's easiest, issues a rule that has to be followed. That gets me pissed off. My father doesn't even know the best times I've had this summer are after 12.

I'm not sure I gave my father enough credit—of course he knew that the best times I'd had all summer were after midnight. That's what he was trying to prevent—too much "best times." The truth was, I wasn't getting into much trouble. The only thing my friends and I were drunk on was self-absorption. We would stay out late and go up to the cemetery, where we'd lay on our backs on the grass, looking up at the stars and talking about the meaning of life and our place in it. We didn't care about the future, only the present.

We make very unreasonable demands on high school seniors. This is the time when we expect kids to decide on college and begin planning their lives. Of course, there is no worse time for them to be doing this. For all of senior year, you're living in the minute to minute, and the only voice you hear is your own. It's as if you have headphones on and they're blasting your own thoughts back at you at full volume. Your teachers sound like Charlie Brown's did, and your parents are just background noise.

As I said, my parents gave me a lot of latitude as I experimented with my persona as a teen, but that last year of high school I would put their hands-off approach to the test by pushing my nights later and later.

The next chapter in my romantic life began almost by accident at the Women's Community Committee Thrift Shop during one of their famous Brown Bag Sales. At these sales, you could take anything you could fit into a big brown paper sack for five dollars. That particular day I spotted a beautiful After Six tuxedo jacket, along with the matching pants, complete with the silk stripe down the side. I tried it on—and it was a 38 regular, just my size.

"That one is not part of the bag sale," said the woman from the Women's Community Committee. "That suit is eight dollars."

That was at the upper end of my budget, but I had to have it. I filled two brown bags and with the tux spent eighteen dollars. That purchase gave me the motivation. Now that I had a tuxedo, I was going to have to take that After Six to some dances.

There were many kinds of dance social events throughout the school year. Of course there was the senior prom, and the junior prom, but there were also the class semiformals in the fall, and the band semiformal since the "bandies" had to have their own social event, too. So there were plenty of ways to put that old tux to work and I planned to do it.

The senior semiformal was coming up, so I started with the Ally Sheedy of the art room. My progress, or lack thereof, is all down in black and white in my diary:

> I saw Susan Brady after the achievement tests. Talking to her always sparks some curiosity in my mind as to whether or not she likes me or not.
>
> Either she doesn't care at all, or she wants me to think that she doesn't care.

And then the very next entry:

> Susan didn't care. After she told me she didn't want to go out with me, she said she did not want to "dissolve our relationship completely." I could accept that and continued calling her. But

now I realize that her mind is closed. My present situation with Jennifer is very strange. I've known her for so long. But I haven't been attracted to her until now. I'm not sure why.

I don't know if I really lacked this much self-awareness or not. But I guess I didn't want to admit I'd put Jennifer, my Molly Ringwald, firmly in second place, and she was going to be my rebound. But she was a shoo-in, as far as I was concerned. I asked her to the semiformal.

"Um, I'm actually going into Boston that night, to a club," Jennifer said. "I'm going to see Dicky's band. Did you know? I'm kind of going out with him now."

I couldn't believe it. I had waited too long and I lost out to Dicky Barrett. Meanwhile, Catherine looked at me like a Labrador every day. She was there for the taking. Catherine, the only one who *really* liked me, had waited so patiently for me to come around. But could I give her the satisfaction? Of course not. Ego bruised, I had to look elsewhere. Look at this next entry:

> *I asked Ann Pink to the senior semi-formal Friday. She's making me wait until tomorrow for an answer. It's really been on my mind this weekend.*
>
> *Catherine asked me to the semi-formal and I said no. I don't like turning people down, especially one I like, like her. She really bummed out over the rejection. But I can't do much about it. I'm still her friend.*

What a heel I was! But it's nice to see that after I tossed her aside I was willing to unilaterally announce that I was still her friend. Let's see what happened on Monday:

> *Today was a big day. It really blew my mind. Ann Pink said she wanted to go to the prom with me, but could not give me an immediate answer. I wondered why, but then I found out it was Mitiguy that was interfering in my affairs. I talked to him about it and he said "Don't worry, Tom. If you asked her, you're going with her. I'll back off." He immediately went to her and asked her. She said yes!*

Mitiguy! My childhood chum had returned, unexpectedly, to stick a shiv into my social life. He always was a devious one.

So, I gave in and went to the senior semiformal with Catherine, and I was lucky she would still go with me after what I'd done to string her along. But I was still keeping her in the friend-zone, and decided to use the dance as an opportunity to solidify my reputation as an outsider. When I showed up at Catherine's apartment I was wearing outrageous Goth makeup that made me look like Robert Smith from the Cure. I had my hair slicked back and was wearing black eyeliner and black lipstick. Of course I didn't fix myself up like this at home—my dad would have locked the door and my mother would have begun praying the Rosary. I took my supplies with me to the parking lot of Building 19 on Route 1 and made myself up in the reflection of the rearview mirror of my mother's 1979 Chevy Monza.

When she opened her door, Catherine was horrified but tried not to show it. Her father was more horrified and had no trouble showing it. When he took our photo, his face was paler than mine.

I caused a stir at the semiformal. I was weird, and I got the attention I was looking for—posing for photos, dancing with myself to the song "Dancing With Myself." I should have been ashamed of myself, and looking back now, I am. I'd made it all about me, but Catherine was forgiving. She'd had a crush on me in the art room for months, so I could do no wrong. She was just glad I'd finally said yes to her. She was as sweet a date as I'd ever had, just adoring and adorable.

After ruining her prom, I thought I owed her, so I took her out for an afternoon date at Liggett's Drug Store. I thought this could be where we'd become "friends." They had a lunch counter and we drank coffee out of cups and saucers and ate lemon meringue pie. Catherine made conversation with the old people at the counter. She was a little odd, it turned out. We laughed a lot. Before we left, Catherine promised the retirees we'd come back the next day, so we did, and spent another afternoon laughing at the lunch counter.

She snuck up on me. A few weeks later, this girl I kept in third place forever became my surprise girlfriend. We'd go on dates in the dead of winter and we'd kiss in my car with the engine running in front of her apartment building until thirty minutes after her curfew. We went to see the movie *A Christmas Story* at the Needham Cinema and held hands. Then we went out for ice cream sundaes and looked into each other's eyes. I was in love with her before I knew it. I hadn't even given myself permission.

The fact was I fell for Catherine so fast because she was outrageous. She was deep and moody and philosophical. We would take long walks and sit under weeping willow trees and talk about God, love, life, and death. She could change her mood in an instant. She'd be laughing and then, suddenly, would just burst into tears. She kept me off balance. It scared me, but it pulled me in. I loved the feelings but I was a little put off by them. They went against the image I had for myself, as a court jester, who glided through life and kept things light. I liked my lightness, but Catherine made things heavy.

Catherine was now my serious girlfriend, but I still had that senior self-absorption going on. One Friday night Jennifer's parents were away and she invited a bunch of the "art majors" over for a party. Catherine wanted me to go with her, but I told her to go by herself and I would meet her there—I was determined to arrive as an individual, not as a couple.

When I got to Jennifer's house, Catherine was there, but she didn't say hello to me. She had a kind of hollow expression, and when I saw her I remember thinking that she looked like a sleepwalker, like she had just seen a ghost. I thought she was a little miffed that I had wanted to arrive alone. I went to another room to see who was at the party and say my hellos. When I returned a few minutes later she was gone. I looked around for her.

"Oh, she's gone," I was told. "She was acting weird. She left." So I got in my mom's car and drove out to find her.

This is what I wrote about that night in my diary:

> *March 14th, I must say, Catherine is really the best thing I've had in my life. Just looking at her photograph right now makes me feel a lot of things. Last night, she had what I think is called a nervous breakdown. What a scary word. It looks scary just to write it. I was at the party. I ran out. I saw her walking down the side of the road very fast looking straight ahead, not focusing on anything. I pulled my car up on the island. I got out and ran to her, but she didn't turn her head. I had to grab her arm. She began crying immediately.*
>
> *I hugged her and asked her why, why she didn't look at me, why she wasn't talking to me. "I don't know," she said. She must*

have said that 15 times straight in a row. She went on and on
talking about how she hated parties, hated this and that, and was
afraid of the moon because it was cut in half. When I heard her
talk like that, I was definitely scared. I didn't know what to think.
If somebody else had heard her they would have been sure that she
was mentally ill. Technically, she might be. So, I stayed out with
her all that night.

I knew something was very wrong with her, but I didn't
know exactly what. I got her back in the car and drove and
rolled the windows down, letting the cool air blow on us.
I thought to myself, maybe if she gets some fresh air, it will
wake her up and she will snap out of it. When it got too cold, I
rolled up the windows, and Catherine began to talk in very fast
bursts. She made no sense to me. I rolled the windows down
again and let the cold air rush through the car. Although I
wasn't sure why, I put a lot of faith in fresh air.

Eventually I drove back to my house and parked in my
driveway. I turned off the engine and focused on her. I tried to
listen.

Her fast talking become slow talking, and eventually she
put her head on my shoulder and fell asleep for a few minutes
at a time. Then she'd wake up and start talking again. I stayed
in the Chevy Monza with her in my driveway until sunrise.
By then she was calm, and we were both delirious. I thought
about taking her into my kitchen and making her some breakfast, explaining everything to my parents, but I wasn't sure I
knew enough about what was happening to explain anything.
I should have done this. Instead, I backed the car up and pulled
away, and drove her home. I walked her to her door and told
her to get some rest. She promised she would. I didn't kiss her

good-bye. She slipped in quietly and closed the door behind her. Maybe she would sleep it all off, I thought. Maybe it was all over. But I knew it wasn't.

When I returned home my parents were in their bathrobes making coffee in the kitchen. My father wanted to know where the hell I had been all night. And what the hell I thought I was doing. That we'd been over this before and that he'd said no more late nights. I understood his ire.

"I was in the driveway until about thirty minutes ago," I said.

"You were in our driveway?"

"Just sitting there, with Catherine. We were talking."

"And you stayed here in our driveway, just talking until seven in the morning and you just drove her home . . . that's your story?"

"Yeah."

"I don't believe it, but it doesn't matter because you're not going out again. You're done."

My mother was puzzled. "You were in our driveway? What were you doing out there?" she asked.

"Go to bed," said my dad, cutting her off. He thought he had a pretty good idea of what I was doing out there all night. Probably something that resembled the lyrics of a certain Meat Loaf song. I wanted to correct the record, but felt I couldn't because I would have had to explain what had happened to Catherine, and I wasn't sure myself. It was too complicated. I went upstairs to sleep. Maybe when I woke up the whole thing would be over, and I could just be grounded like a normal kid.

When I woke up it was noon and I had to get to a choral concert at a nearby junior high school, so I put on a hot-pink shirt buttoned to the top and my tux jacket and went off to the concert. But before the concert I drove to Catherine's. She was awake and alone. Catherine was writing and sketching on a big pad of paper, and trying to explain some theory, something that seemed a little crazy. But I didn't have time to think about her sketches—I had to get to my concert. I told Catherine to come with me; we got in my car and drove to the school. I walked her into the auditorium and found her a seat.

I was a little late to the music room, but my director didn't say anything. I was supposed to wear black and white, but I had worn the hot-pink shirt. I really don't know why I had made that decision. I suddenly had no desire whatsoever to stand out and be different. *Why did I need attention all the time? What good was it?* All of a sudden I didn't want to be unique or exciting or radical or anything at all. I just wanted to be normal, and I wanted Catherine to be normal when that concert was over.

While we were singing I noticed Catherine get up out of her seat and walk out of the auditorium. I tried to concentrate on the music for the last few songs, but it was nearly impossible, and as soon as the curtain closed I raced off stage left and began searching for her. I went into the choral room, the art room, and then walked down the hallway where I spotted her in the band room. She was rearranging everything, placing the chairs and the instruments in a new configuration. They were in neat rows, the two sections facing each other. Some of the music stands were arranged flat, with their trays horizontal; some were standing vertical. It was all very deliberate.

"These have to be this way," she said. "They are better this way. Everything will sound better this way."

"Catherine, we have to go," I said.

She looked into my eyes, reassuringly, and said, "I liked the way you sang." I felt humbled by her compliment, mostly because, at that moment, she looked so at peace, so wise. All of a sudden I felt like the manic one, trying so desperately to figure out what had Catherine change and become moody. She was fine now—I was the one on edge.

Some of the other kids in the chorus were walking by the room, looking in at us. I felt as if I was about to be caught, figured out, so I left the chairs in their strange configuration and walked Catherine to my car.

I did some more driving around with the windows down. I thought it had worked the first night, but its power was waning. She looked exhausted, so I took her home again. I continued to keep her condition, and my worries about her, a secret.

I went to her apartment again a few days later without a plan. I thought about my options—perhaps another one of my windy drives. It was still the only remedy at my disposal. Catherine stuck her head out of her door like a squirrel and motioned "Come in" with her hand, then darted back inside, leaving the door open. I went inside and she was standing in the middle of her living room. She had all the shades pulled down. The song "Red, Red Wine" by UB40 was playing softly. Catherine had filled everything glass in her apartment that could hold liquid with red-colored water. All the glasses, bowls, jars—anything glass.

"They're clean. Everything's clean," she said with conviction.

This was it. If I doubted it before, I was now sure. She was not well. She had gone crazy, or she was in the midst of some kind of crazy spell. My heart was pounding, but I didn't want to upset the mood she had set: various candles glowed behind her, which she had also carefully arranged.

"It looks nice," I said. "Did it take a long time?"

"No, not at all," she said, looking at me puzzled. "Not at all. It had to be done. I had to do it. It was easy. I love this song, don't you? It helped me sleep last night."

I moved to the couch and we both sat and talked for a while. Mostly I listened to her talk; she still had many theories to parse. I noticed "Red, Red Wine" was on endless repeat. She had recorded it as a loop onto a cassette tape. Whatever was happening with her, it was certainly making her very resourceful. I wondered about my next move. Could a boyfriend check a girlfriend into a mental hospital?

Then her dad walked in. He'd been out all day and this was the first he'd seen of her "red" project.

"What in God's name is going on? Goddamnit! What in GOD'S NAME?" he screamed.

"Don't pour it out, Dad. It's cleaning everything. Everything has to be cleaned!"

"You are talking nonsense, and it's going to stop! You've been talking nonsense for two days straight. You're going to clean all this up right now!"

"I can't clean up yet. Not until everything's clean," she explained.

He walked right up to her in the middle of the room. "Snap! The HELL! OUT OF IT!" he yelled, slapping her hard across the face. I stood up but I didn't move from my spot. I wanted to run and grab him and be the hero, but I froze.

Catherine looked down to the floor and held her cheek. She didn't look scared or upset, but like she was thinking intently on a math problem. Then she calmly walked to her bedroom.

"Goddamnit!" he said. "Look at this place!"

"I can help clean this up," I offered.

"No, you go. I'll do it."

"She needs help," I blurted out. He looked at me, and his face softened immediately. "I think she needs help," I repeated.

He took a deep breath and muttered, "Yeah."

*

Three days later the doctor called me at home and asked me to come in. When I went in to the hospital, Catherine's family was sitting in the downstairs lobby. I awkwardly told them I was going up to meet with the doctor.

The doctor had a beautiful, spacious office. She told me that Catherine had experienced a very serious breakdown, and she was going to need a long stay in the hospital, but that she would get better. "Based on the work we've done with her, and her writing, you are a source of calm in her life right now, and we would love to make you part of her recovery. Would you be comfortable with that?"

"Absolutely," I said. I felt so relieved. I'd never liked hospitals, but this hospital seemed like a beautiful place. A weight had lifted off my shoulders. There was now a whole ward of professionals who were able to do what I thought was an impossible task just a few days before.

"I'm going to take you in to see her. She is heavily medicated, so it may be a shock to see her in this state. She's going to be lethargic, but these drugs are needed to help her remain calm and rest."

She was sitting in an easy chair in the psych ward when I walked in. She was barely there. She managed a smile when she saw me, but her eyelids were half closed. If I had seen her like this a week before, I would have been horrified. But now I was just glad she was safe.

Before I left that day, I met with the doctor again. She asked if we could set up a schedule for me to come every day after school to visit, which I was more than happy to do. I felt completely up to the task. I wanted to be of help in any way I could. I would have expected to feel burdened by the responsibility, but it was just the opposite. I was thrilled to be relieved of the ugly burden of self-absorption. All I'd done for two years was think about myself.

I went home and told my parents everything. About the nervous breakdown, about why I stayed out all night in the driveway with Catherine. About why I'd been sneaking around and taking her for drives, about why I'd been afraid to tell them anything. In what shouldn't have come as a surprise to me, but did at the time, they were completely understanding. When I finished, my dad put his hand on my shoulder. He didn't say anything, and I didn't want him to. He understood. I welled up, nodded my head, and walked to my room. I didn't burst out crying until I got to the top of the stairs. I slept well for the first time in days.

When I woke up everything was different. I was so grateful for the support of my parents, for Catherine's doctor, and for the support of the whole mental health establishment. Adults were pretty cool! I was done with my immature need to be alternative, to strive for attention and push the envelope. How nice it was for those weeks and months to think about nothing except the well-being of another person.

Catherine and I didn't last forever obviously, but I was

there as she got better. And she did get better. While I know I was of help to her during that brief period in her life, she probably helped me more in the long run. I look at my time with her as the beginning of my adulthood, when I first learned to look beyond myself.

CHAPTER 20

BE A (SLIGHTLY NAÏVE) JOKER

SO SOMEWHERE ALONG THE LINE I DECIDED TO BE-come a comedian. I should explain how that hap-pened, I suppose.

Comedians are often assumed to be tortured souls, or sad clowns, people who were desperately driven to a life making jokes because of their own deep-seeded insecurity, their need to please others because they had overbearing parents, be-cause they were hurt or ignored as a child and need constant attention, or due to an insatiable desire to hide their pain with humor. That's not quite me, since my childhood was pretty normal and pretty happy. But I was definitely looking for an outlet to express myself, and I definitely liked the limelight. Perhaps comedy came along at the right time. While I was leading my very serious life outside of school with Catherine, I became embroiled in something that will forever be referred to by all who know me as:

The Gong Show Scandal

It began, as most of my stories do, at home.

As kids we were allowed to watch TV but the content we consumed was regulated by a small agency in the office in our basement. My dad would watch TV down there, and keep an ear on what was playing upstairs in the living room. He didn't wait for a "viewer discretion is advised" warning; he would decide on his own whether or not something was appropriate. Certain TV shows we knew were automatically off-limits: *Maude* (glorified divorce), *The Love Boat* (wrong kind of love), *Dallas*, and *Dynasty* (trash).

We'd hear through the floor that his TV had tuned to the same station we were watching, and we knew our show was "under review." If after a few minutes he didn't like what he saw, he'd come upstairs, walk in the living room, and slap the TV's ON button with the palm of his hand. The picture would go dark, Dad would go back downstairs, and we'd be left sitting in a silent room. We'd grab books.

My dad used to make us watch all his favorite old movies. Especially musicals. He never sang a note or performed himself, but he was a passionate viewer. He'd announce from below "*Kiss Me Kate* is on channel five!" and we knew that was the only option for TV that night. He loved all the Rodgers and Hammerstein Technicolor musicals—*Oklahoma!, Carousel, The King and I, State Fair,* and *South Pacific*—and wanted to make sure we loved them, too. Most of these were shown on network TV once a year, and we were expected to watch them every time.

He loved comedy teams like Laurel and Hardy and Abbott

and Costello, and duets like "Brush Up Your Shakespeare" from *Kiss Me, Kate!* He always implored me to "watch these guys . . . it's all about the timing! The timing is the most important part!"

If this were today, he'd probably be forcing us to watch DVDs and Turner Classic Movies, but as it was, we could only watch what came on TV. Still, he showed impatience when his children weren't familiar with his favorites. "You never saw *Angels with Dirty Faces*? Rosemary, did you hear this? These kids have never seen *Angels with Dirty Faces*! What's the matter with you!?" I would just shrug my shoulders, but I probably should have said, "Dad, it's the 1970s and the options for viewing *Angels with Dirty Faces* are extremely limited."

But all through my childhood I was exposed to so much of this classic entertainment, the greats like Bing Crosby, Fred Astaire, Gene Kelly, and the great leading ladies like Ginger Rogers, Jean Arthur, and Katharine Hepburn.

We also watched modern shows, mostly the variety shows that were so popular in the '70s like *Flip Wilson, Hee Haw, Donny & Marie, Mac Davis*, and especially *Carol Burnett*. We loved watching the *Carol Burnett Show*; the whole family could watch and laugh together. There is almost nothing like that on television today—a comedy show that makes everyone laugh, regardless of age. But in those days, everything we watched, whether it was classic screwball comedy films, epics like *Ben-Hur*, variety shows, or dramas like *The Waltons*, it was all "fun for the whole family."

Because of all the entertainment I was raised on, I was ready that senior year of high school to put my education to good use when it came time for the annual Gong Show. As I said, there was no theater department at our school—the only theatrical outlet of any kind at Norwood High was the Senior Gong Show.

The TV show *The Gong Show* with Chuck Barris was a national phenomenon during this time, and I'd venture to guess that most high schools in the 1980s did some version of *The Gong Show* on stage during that decade. For those readers who aren't familiar, *The Gong Show* followed a simple format— talented hopefuls performed, and if they didn't please the audience and the judges, a gong would be sounded, leading to mortification for the performer and hilarity for the audience, especially if the gong went off only seconds into their act. Ours was an annual tradition at Norwood High, and the lucky guy selected as host was generally considered the funniest guy, the class clown. And if you're wondering, yes, up to that point it was always guys. The glass ceiling, as it turned out, was to be broken the following year by none other than my art room flame Jennifer Wheeler (yes, Molly Ringwald!). The job of Gong Show host usually went to a big-man-on-campus type—one of the popular ones, one of the class clowns with a big personality. I had seen the Senior Gong Show several times as an underclassman, and I'd always think to myself, *I could really nail that*. But once I got to my senior year, I wasn't so sure that I was going to be "that guy." I just wasn't popular enough.

But when it came time to audition, I went back to my roots of classic entertainment. I went down to the Norwood Public Library and memorized a few routines from the comedy albums that were available in their collection. I selected one of Bob Newhart's famous one-sided "telephone conversations," where he, as the head of the East India Company, speaks with

Sir Walter Raleigh in the New World as he tried to wrap his mind around Raleigh's enthusiasm for tobacco.

> SPEAKING INTO THE PHONE:
> What you got for us this time, Walt, you got another winner for us?
>
> . . .
>
> Tob-acco . . . er, what's tob-acco, Walt? . . .
>
> . . .
>
> It's a kind of leaf, huh? . . .

Classic routines like this work with any audience. Years later, as an adult, I went to see Bob Newhart live at Carnegie Hall (June 12, 1998) and as an encore he performed a few of his vintage bits: "King Kong," where a security guard on his first day on the job at the Empire State Building speaks by phone to his supervisor about an unforeseen problem; and "Women Drivers," which despite its antiquated title and boldly retro perspective, got huge laughs from an audience of Manhattan elites.

I did the Sir Walter Raleigh routine word for word for Mr. Fuccillo (Mr. Fooch), the math teacher who was faculty advisor for the Gong Show, and when I finished he said to me, "Shillue . . . you might be our Chucky this year. I got a feeling about you. . . . It's an odd choice but I think it might work."

I was an odd choice. But the nerdy attention to detail I had brought to that old-school routine impressed him enough so that he made his decision straightaway. I was shocked but I didn't have time for false modesty. "I'd be all over it," I said.

I did a lot of prep work for my role as host of the Gong Show. Because of the popularity of the TV show, the running gags were built in and all you had to do was ape the character that Chuck Barris had created. He wore a different zany hat each time he came out to introduce a new act, he told bad jokes punctuated by rim shots on the drums, and he would be overly sympathetic to the losing acts. "Why, oh why," he would ask the judges, feigning genuine concern, "did you gong this adorable and talented creature?"

I knew I could put on a good show. I had seen what worked in previous years. But I had a vision for myself, too: I wanted to use these elements and then build upon them to make the show my own. If it seems I was taking the role of talent show host very seriously, I was. When you're in high school, that's the only world that matters. I saw the Gong Show as a great opportunity to put a stamp on the Shillue high school experience. This show would be the closing scene on my teen movie, so I knew I had better get it right, and do it my way.

Obviously, the teen-movie lens we all were using in the 1980s was the work of filmmaker Mr. John Hughes. We watched his movies and thought that our lives ought to measure up to those we saw on screen, even though we knew they were fictional. We didn't have Instagram or Pinterest to use as a scrapbook for our adolescent experience, plotting out the highlights to brag to our friends in competitive ways. We had the John Hughes movie, and I was in the final act. But here's the thing: I wasn't worried about anything. I had nothing to lose. After my ordeal with Catherine, and spending every day at the hospital with her after school, all of the little high school dramas seemed small and insignificant. I was focused.

In planning what would become my stand-up debut, I did what many comedians have done in some form or another at the beginning of their careers: I stole material. My plan wasn't to plagiarize really, but to present classic routines as a tribute, basically a comedy cover-act. But there is no harm in that, and in fact I would recommend it. There is no better way to learn than with good material. So in addition to the purloined routine from Bob Newhart, I also spent weeks learning Rich Little's famous "The Big Game" from the LP *The First Family Rides Again* from 1981. It's a vocal impression tour de force depicting a fictitious poker game that Reagan hosts at the White House with Nixon, Ford, and Carter. Like the Bob Newhart monologue, I took the record to the listening room at the library and played it over and over, transcribing it onto a yellow legal pad. I then took my script home and learned it line for line, and although my impressions weren't very good, the jokes were solid and based on broad caricatures of what Americans thought of the current and former presidents:

> NIXON: Sit down, Gerry. Let's get this show on the road.
> REAGAN: Well, all right. Now the name of the game is draw poker.
> CARTER: I fold!
> REAGAN: I didn't deal the cards yet, Jimmy.

As a comedy routine it still holds up. It's simple, tight, universal, and hilarious, especially when it is delivered by someone as skilled as Rich Little.

As I learned the script line for line, I began to appreciate how the routine builds. No words are wasted, the lines are short and to the point. I learned about the crucial impact of that mysterious thing my dad was always talking about, timing. You had to deliver punch lines at just the right moment to create maximum impact. You can pause sometimes, if you need the audience to make a quick connection, but "slow build" doesn't really work in stand-up. The best punch lines are delivered just as the audience is already figuring it out for themselves. It's like getting the entire audience to sneeze at the same time. It takes great skill to pull off something like this. I pored over these routines and worked them to death. I knew I'd stumbled on to something big. I loved this stuff. I knew I'd never be able to stop doing it.

As the show approached, my faculty advisors, Mr. Fuccillo and Miss Dyer, gave me tips and offered a bunch of recycled jokes that had been used in past years. I remembered many of those jokes and didn't want to repeat them, but I asked them to keep the jokes coming just in case there was something good. I also found some joke books at the library, such as *The Toast-master Generals Favorite Jokes* by George Jessel, and *Doc Blakely's Handbook of Wit and Pungent Humor.* Unsurprisingly, 99 percent of what I found in these tomes was not suitable for my purposes, because they either took too long to set up or took place in a doctor's office in 1958 (too retro even for old-fashioned Tom Shillue!).

At a rehearsal one day, Miss Dyer approached me when I was alone. She whispered to me, "Here's one you can use. . . . Mr. Fuccillo was so lonely in high school, he used to go to the drive-in movie alone and do push-ups in the back seat of his car."

I wrote it down. It didn't seem that funny to me, but it was short and punchy and Miss Dyer seemed to think it was hilarious. So I wrote it down, with the intention of figuring it out later, and using it only if I needed it.

Along with all the comedy material, I prepared a couple of songs with my barbershop quartet, the Boys Next Door. We'd been singing in the bathroom and the stairwells for months and I thought it was time to debut the group in front of an audience.

The night of the show arrived, and it was a packed house, as usual. But, for the first time, the show was going to be simulcast on local cable TV, so there was a production van parked outside the exit door, and three cameras in the auditorium. There was a buzz of small-town excitement in the air.

All the amateur acts on the show got a warm reception. Of course they did—it was a filled-to-capacity audience full of friends and family. You have to remember, this was pre-*American Idol* America, so the standards were pretty low. If you could get through "Once, Twice, Three Times a Lady" and end in the same key you started in, you were considered a prodigy, and shipped off to conservatory school, blissfully unaware you were embarking on a bright future in the service industry. This is why I don't find it at all sad when Simon Cowell makes some fifteen-year-old cry in front of her shocked family and all of America. Much better to have your dreams crushed when you are young and resilient. Trust me, those crying *American Idol* kids are back playing soccer and laughing with their friends a week later. Or they should be. I think the "Once, Twice, Three Times a Lady" guy I went to high school with is now working at Guitar Center.

The vast majority of the students in the show, however, were just there to have a good time. Most of the acts in the Senior Gong Show were just kids matching their lip movements to prerecorded music. (The term *lip-sync* was not yet common usage in the '80s—a bunch of guys doing an air-guitar version of "Brown Sugar" was listed in the program as "A Pantomime of the Rolling Stones." How quaint.)

And of course there was the requisite dance number where the boys' football team dressed in drag and did a kickline dance to whoops and hollers from the audience. I'm sure there wasn't a town in America whose high school variety show in the 1980s didn't include a showstopping number where jocks donned skirts and pranced around to "Girls Just Want to Have Fun."

I still remember the experience of hosting the show vividly—the funny hats and the generic jokes worked as I expected them to, since these were the familiar touchstones that everyone who watched the television version of *The Gong Show* knew. But my ad-libs in between acts were getting unexpected laughs, and this was the real thrill for me. *I was getting organic laughs by bantering with the audience.* This is where I made a decision right there on the stage to abandon my "acquired" material. I ditched the Bob Newhart and Rich Little routines I'd worked so hard on and decided to go it alone. This was the first time in my life I was in command of a crowd, and I wanted it to be all me. It was a very powerful feeling and I knew I wouldn't forget it. If you hear comedians talking about their first good crowd, it sounds a lot like addicts talking about the first time they smoked meth or snorted a line of coke. I imagine the feelings are very similar—especially the sense that there is no going back.

Halfway through I tried some of my original material. I did some impressions of the principal and vice principal. They did the morning announcements over the PA every day, and every student was familiar with their cadence. The principal, Mr. Piccirilli, always began by tapping three times on the microphone and saying, "Could I have your attention please."

Using the handheld microphone I unremarkably re-created

the *tap, tap, tap* . . . and brought down the house. I moved on to the vice principal, Mr. Usevich. He talked loud, so I talked loud . . . boom, easy laughs. Since I now had the crowd in the palm of my hand, I continued. Mr. Murphy, the phys. ed. teacher, was standing at the side of the auditorium; I suppose he was acting as a chaperone in some capacity, but I had no idea he was going to be there. Mr. Murphy was a very popular, very good-looking young guy, and in great shape, but he had a bald spot on the top of his head. Perhaps because he was considered such a "hunk" in every other way, students felt very comfortable teasing him about his bald spot, and he always seemed to be a good sport about it. Coming off my roasting of the administration, I thought I would ad-lib a line about him.

"Mr. Murphy is here . . . Hey, could we turn down the lights in this area [gesturing to Mr. Murphy and squinting], they're kind of reflecting off Mr. Murphy's head."

I wasn't prepared for the response. A huge burst of laughter, mixed with "Ooohh"s and "Aaah"s. It wasn't even a good roast joke; it was a bit rambling. But as Mr. Murphy, his face now red, smiled and nodded, the crowd continued to laugh. They loved it, so of course I continued. Then I recalled the joke Miss Dyer had given me. It was buried in the back of my cue cards, but I was able to recite it from memory.

"You know, Mr. Murphy was so lonely in high school . . . he used to go to drive-in movies and do push-ups in the back seat of his car."

The audience absolutely exploded. I can't describe the cacophony that followed. I still didn't find the joke that funny, but the crowd was losing it. They were shrieking, and howling, and looking at each other like they couldn't believe what I'd said. It was very strange, but I wasn't going to argue with a big laugh. I stood there smirking like a pro, trying to milk it the way Johnnie Carson did, looking from side to side at no one in particular as if to say, "I don't even know what I just said!" But the reality was, I didn't. I thought I had made a joke about a guy doing push-ups.

It took a while for the crowd to quiet down, and as I moved on to announcing another act, I could see the principal, Mr. Piccirilli running down the side aisle and speaking in an animated fashion with one of the guys manning the public access TV cameras. He didn't look happy, and for a moment I thought he might be upset about the bald joke; he was probably not aware that it was a running gag at school, and that Mr. Murphy was totally cool with it. Anyway, what did I care? I was owning the stage just then.

Like most scandals, the Norwood High Gong Show Scandal took a while to brew. I had heard over the weekend that there was some type of "power outage" during the cable broadcast of the show, and only part of it had aired. I wasn't aware of the real story, which was that after my roast of Mr. Murphy, Mr. Piccirilli had, in fact, stopped the public access broadcast and confiscated the videotapes of the show. I was called into his office bright and early on Monday morning. As I was walking into the office, Mr. Fooch and Miss Dyer were walking out, and they had grave expressions on their faces.

Mr. Piccirilli told me that he had destroyed the videotape of the show and he was embarrassed for the parents and families who were in attendance. He assured me that it was not my impressions of him and the vice principal that were at issue.

"We have good senses of humor and we can take it. It was

the remark that you made about Mr. Murphy that was, frankly, way out of line."

I tried to reassure him. "Oh, Mr. Murphy doesn't mind. We joke about that all the time with him."

I still thought we were talking about the bald joke.

"You say that kind of thing to teachers at this school?"

"Just Mr. Murphy. And maybe Mr. Cooper. They're both okay with it, so I thought it would be fine."

"It's not fine! It's obscene!"

I couldn't believe he was getting so worked up, and my bewilderment was making Mr. Piccirilli all the more agitated.

"I hope you realize you've put the future of this show in jeopardy! We allowed you a forum in which to entertain your classmates, and you obviously thought you could take advantage of that. But I would say at the very least, you owe an apology to Mr. Murphy, and I expect you to go do that right now."

"Okay. I'll do that. Thank you."

He seemed genuinely puzzled at my lack of contrition as I left.

I went to Mr. Murphy's office and told him I was sorry.

"That's all right, I can take it," he said.

"I thought it would be okay because you've made jokes about your hair in gym class."

"I don't think it was the bald joke that got you in hot water, buddy. I'm pretty sure it was the line about the push-ups in the car!" Mr. Murphy burst out laughing.

"Oh. Okay."

"I mean I gotta hand it to you, Shillue. That was ballsy!"

Apparently the joke wasn't about physical fitness. I thought about it all afternoon. I still didn't get it. And then, it started to dawn on me why the principal got so worked up. Clearly the joke had to be something about sex. Why else would he get so angry? So the push-ups were simulating sex? Was that it? It seemed like a stretch to me. I was still hazy.

It was only recently that I discovered the joke originally came from Rodney Dangerfield. Here's his version: *When I was a kid, everyone thought I got plenty of girls. I'd go to a drive-in movie and do push-ups in the back seat of my car.*

Now that version is a little easier to understand. Maybe if I had heard Rodney perform it, I would have gotten the sexual implications at the time. But here's the thing: even though I hadn't meant it that way, everyone was treating me like I had. Word got all around the school of the reaction to the scandal, and the aborted cable TV broadcast, and students were whispering about the joke to each other and laughing at their lockers. Teachers were shaking their heads at me as I passed, but they were smiling. They thought my joke was funny.

I decided to stay silent about my naïveté and embrace my new comedic persona.

I guess the adage that there is no such thing as bad publicity applied. In the course of a few days I'd gone through all the essential elements of a show biz career: discovery, accolades, scandal, and gossip. And I survived. I was like a Gloria Gaynor song.

The irony is, if I had been more streetwise and understood the joke, I would have been too afraid to do it. My innocence and naïveté had given the joke much more kick because it was so unexpected. And my lack of contrition that followed just blew the whole thing up even further. Another benefit to my sheltered, chaste lifestyle as a teen! You see? Abstinence makes you edgier.

After all I had been through with my girlfriend, and now this newfound love of comedy, as well as the scandal, I knew I would no longer be content as an awkward art room kid. I was too experienced now. I'd seen and done too much. I liked my new identity as a worldly, comic leading man much better.

Puffed up with the confidence of my debut performance, I decided to go into Boston to a comedy club to get the lay of this new land. I went to Nick's Comedy Stop in the theater district, on the edge of what used to be called the Combat Zone. If anyone knows about the comedy scene in Boston in the mid-1980s, you know that it is a long way from the Norwood High School auditorium. I was underage but walked right past the bouncers on the way in. I guess there weren't many underage kids trying to get into a comedy show all by themselves. The place had the feel of a Vegas showroom—brass fixtures lined the stage; the booths were dark-red vinyl—the lineup was a who's who of 1980s Boston Comedy. All the comedians were fast, loud, dirty, and hilarious. And very Boston. Their acts had a confrontational, hard edge to them. I thought, *I can't do anything like this*. I grew up in Norwood. I was an altar boy. My comedy role models are Bob Newhart and Tim Conway. I had an image of myself doing a quiet act in a double-breasted blazer, full of wordplay and pregnant pauses. That would never fly at a place like this. I needed a Plan B.

CHAPTER 21

B♭ MINOR

SO I LEFT HIGH SCHOOL WITH NO ACT, AND MINIMAL performance experience, but a dream to be on stage. Well, if the modern world of stand-up comedy was too hard-edged for my old-fashioned style, I had to figure out another avenue. And it just so happened that I did have another artistic pursuit, one that couldn't be more fitting to my wholesome image—my barbershop quartet, the Boys Next Door. By any objective standard my group was pretty darn good. We did well whether it was in front of a friendly audience at school or on the street singing in front of a bunch of strangers in Harvard Square. We basically crushed it at every one of our unpaid performances.

I was struck with the brilliant idea that my barbershop quartet could be my ticket into show business. In hindsight it seems incredibly naïve, of course, to think that I would get famous as part of a barbershop quartet, but I believed I was just thinking outside the box, and that was going to make all the difference. After all, at the time Steve Martin was one of the biggest comedy stars around, and although his albums weren't allowed in my house because they featured a big label that said "EXPLICIT" across it, I used to watch his many appearances on *Saturday Night Live*, playing his banjo and doing absurdist humor with an arrow through his head. I thought I could bring the art of barbershop back and make it hip, the way Steve Martin had when he put his own twist on what was essentially an old-fashioned vaudeville routine.

So, with this in mind, I decided to put together an audition tape for *Saturday Night Live*. I watched the show every week, and I knew I was nothing like Eddie Murphy or Joe Piscopo, but it seemed entirely plausible to me that I might get an audition with my current skill set—I had done a darn good job in the high school Gong Show; I could emcee, tell jokes, and sing barbershop; I was old school—like Jackie Gleason or Danny Kaye. Maybe what the world needed was a throwback like those guys. I thought I deserved a shot at the big time. So I went down to the local public access cable studio, strapped on a lavalier microphone, sat on a stool in front of a white backdrop, and I narrated the introduction to my demo tape.

"Hello, Lorne Michaels. A lot has been said about this young man Tom Shillue. Have you heard of him? Let's have a look. . . ."

Using the massive off-line video editing deck at the public access station, I taught myself to edit from scratch and cut together scenes from the Gong Show: me emceeing, doing impressions of my teachers, and, of course, I finished with what I thought was my ace in the hole, my barbershop quartet. *Who else is going to submit a barbershop quartet to* Saturday Night Live? I thought. *Nobody! That's who!*

After its one and only airing (in order to get free use of the cable equipment, you had to agree to air anything you produced on local cable TV, so at some point that week, they popped my five-minute audition for *Saturday Night Live* into the schedule, probably between a town selectmen's meeting and a broadcast of the high school football game), I sent the VHS tapes not just to Lorne Michaels but also to a handful of folks from the ending credits of the show. I didn't know how important they were; I selected them based on whether or not they had a nice-sounding name. There was even a guy who worked on the show named Tom Shiller. Shiller? Only one letter different from Shillue! I thought at the very least I'd get his attention with my name. I probably sent about ten in all of the carefully packaged and addressed VHS tapes down to 30 Rockefeller Center, New York, New York.

Now what do you do after you send in a résumé for a job? You follow up with a phone call, of course. So a week later I was calling 30 Rock and asking for Lorne Michaels. Keep in mind that I was all of seventeen years old at this point, but I was brimming with the kind of heedless confidence I wish I had today. We should all act like rubes all the time, because we'd get a lot more done and we'd never worry about whether we were doing the "acceptable" thing.

"Tom Shillue for Lorne Michaels!" This was my greeting. Friendly and unhurried, but also with an urgency, as if I had just gotten off the phone with Lorne a few minutes before and had remembered something the minute we hung up, so I needed to call back immediately. In my self-taught crash course in cold calling I quickly learned that when you ask for somebody important on the phone, the person on the other end always asks, "Who's calling?" This presents the first stumbling block. So, to get past this I'd act like someone important who would expect to be put through right away. Of course, this never worked—the receptionist would inevitably follow up with "Does he know you?" to which I'd energetically reply, "I can only hope he does! What's your name?"

The receptionist would usually tell me her name and then proceed to hustle me off the phone, but then I had a name that I could use the next time I called—so it was sort of a win.

"Hi, Darlene, how are you?" I'd say the next time I called. "It's Tom Shillue for Lorne."

I know this approach seems a bit on the delusional spectrum, maybe even a little bit psychopathic—but from my perspective there was absolutely no downside to my behavior. Perhaps Lorne Michaels's personal assistant was rolling her eyes at me from 250 miles away, but I'd never met her, so it didn't matter! Deep in my core, the dork king remained.

After several weeks of aggressively pursuing an audition for *Saturday Night Live* my results appeared to be: not a thing. I had nothing at all to show for all my mailings and cold calls, except the experience itself. Sometimes that's enough: the knowledge that I had tried, even though I had nothing to show for it.

But some stories have unexpected endings.

*

Several weeks later I took the bus into the city to do what so many suburbanites of my age did, walk up and down Newberry Street in the Back Bay, occasionally stopping in one of its many record stores or boutiques to stare long and hard at things I wasn't going to buy. Most of the shops had bulletin boards that catered to the students of the many colleges in the area, and on one I saw a notice:

ENTERTAINERS WANTED.

SINGERS! DANCERS! ACTORS!

SPECIALTY ACTS!

This was a posting for theme parks, looking to hire entertainers for the summer. Well, this seemed too good to be true! I mean, the only amusement park I'd ever been to was Paragon Park at Nantasket Beach, and the only entertainment they had there was Zoltar the animatronic fortune-teller. This posting was for the big parks, places like Busch Gardens. They were casting for entertainment roles in theme parks "all over the U.S.A and Canada!"

I wrote down the date and time of the audition from the poster and found a pay phone to call my baritone, Sponsel Martin.

"Can we get the guys together for this?" I asked.

"Absolutely!" he said.

As barbershop quartets go, we had been pretty busy lately. After we had performed in the talent show at school, we were approached by a member of the audience and invited to be his guest at his organization's next local meeting. The audience member in question was actually the father of my old sweetheart-that-wasn't, Susan (yes, Ally Sheedy's dad!), and he was a member of the Society for the Preservation and Encouragement of Barber Shop Quartet Singing in America, heretofore referred to by its tidy acronym, SPEBSQSA.

We went down to the meeting in the church basement and

sang the two songs we had sung in the show. We didn't think any performance could have gotten us a better reception than we did at the Gong Show, but these guys practically hoisted us up on their shoulders. This room full of old guys lit up—they couldn't have been happier to see a group of kids singing their kind of music. We stayed until late that night with them learning old songs and singing "tags." (For those of you not familiar, a tag is the end of a song, when the group builds to a crescendo, either by one singer holding out a note while the others harmonize around him or all four hitting a big fat chord together. Every quartet likes to put their own special tag on the end of a standard barbershop song, and when quartets get together they teach and trade tags with each other late into the night. They're like the Pokémon of barbershop.)

We joined up the following week and began singing with the Canton Bay–Statesmen SPEBSQSA chorus. They immediately had us fitted for uniforms and proudly stuck us in the front row. We really just wanted to sing in a quartet, but we couldn't resist all the accolades they were throwing at us. They really took the ENCOURAGEMENT part of SPEBSQSA very seriously.

So we assembled our quartet for a Saturday-morning audition at the Grand Hyatt Hotel in Boston. Our quartet didn't really have any uniforms to speak of—we usually just wore a bunch of mismatched three-button sport jackets culled from various Goodwill outlets. But for this "professional" audition I thought we should look as slick as possible, so we used our SPEBSQSA chorus tuxedos. The Canton Bay–Statesmen men's chorus must have scored a good deal on these suits at a fire sale, because they were exceedingly retro. So we were decked out head-to-toe in those mint-green beauties, with dark-green piping on the lapels, and bell-bottomed pants with zip-up boots. Walking through Copley Square on the way to the hotel we looked like four Boy Scouts auditioning to play pimps in a remake of *Shaft*.

We went into the hotel and signed in for our audition spot. This was my first taste of professional show business. Dancers in leg warmers stretched and did pirouettes in the hallway while singers were doing vocal warm-ups in the bathroom. Girls and guys both were decked out in tight sweatpants, hiked up with the waistbands folded down. A lot of the performers seemed to know one another. These were theater people, and here we were, a group of square Irish Catholic kids from a blue-collar, Irish Catholic town. A little bit of that Southie attitude rubs off on anyone from the Boston suburbs, so to us, we were the tough guys in that room. We just stood there leaning against the wall with our hands in our mint-green polyester pockets and waited to be called in. We didn't need any of that warm-up stuff. We knew what we were made of. We would tear the shit out of "You Must've Been a Beautiful Baby" when the time came.

When they finally called for the Boys Next Door, we waltzed in and I pulled out my pitch pipe. To my great surprise there wasn't a table full of casting directors at the end of a big show-room but rather just one round little man sitting at a round table with a bottle of water and a platter with cheese, crackers, and fruit in front of him.

"Hello, boys!" he said, getting up and shaking hands. "I understand you're a barbershop quartet. Well, I don't want to make you nervous, but I'm going to tell you right off the bat, we need a quartet for one of our parks, and if you have what it takes, you might be looking at a full-time job. I like your look. Where'd you get those suits?"

"These are our formal outfits," I said, jumping in. "We use

these for corporate shows, dinner parties, and grand open-ings." We had yet to do any of these things, of course, but the statement was not technically a lie. If we ever did have book-ings like that, these would be the suits we would wear.

"We've also got casual outfits that work better for outdoors and more informal shows."

"Well, I wouldn't worry about that. If you end up working for Show Biz Incorporated, you'll be provided some pretty nice wardrobe. But let's not get ahead of ourselves. Let's hear what you got."

I blew a B natural and we launched into "OH . . . YOU . . . must've been a beautiful baby, cuz baby look at you NOW (you now!)."

"Beautiful Baby" was tight. It was a direct rip-off from our barbershop heroes, the Boston Common. They had won the In-ternational SPEBSQSA Championship in 1980, and we'd even met them at one of the big Northeast District conventions, and cornered them in a hotel lobby so we could sing a song with them. Barbershoppers come from all around to attend these SPEBSQSA conventions for the purpose of competing against other quartets and choruses, but for most the real desire is to hang out, have fun, learn tags, and look for an opportunity to "sing one with the Champs." We had learned every song on the Boston Common's album note for note. We weren't champions but we were doing a pretty darn good imitation of them in that ballroom. At the end, I sing the word "NOW!" and just hold the note, and the other guys echo with the classic descending chromatic barbershop chords "TAKE A LOOK AT YOU . . ." and end it with the big fat major chord "NOW!!!"

His face didn't give anything away, but we could hear the chords. We knew we had impressed him.

"Not bad," he said. "Got anything else?"

I blew a B flat and we cued up our best slow song: "If the Rest of the World Don't Want You, You Will Always Be Welcome Back Home." This sentimental ballad was what barbershop was made for. We had used it to make old ladies cry in *three separate counties*. The climax of the song is "If the rest of the world don't want you . . . then go back to your MOTHER AND DAAAAAAAD!" And when we hit it, we could see Mr. Show Biz must have had kids of his own—parents are much more susceptible to this song than regular people, and when we hit the "DAD" chord, we could see it in his eyes.

We got the job.

*

The Boys Next Door was originally an ironic title for our quartet. We didn't consider ourselves "boys next door" types. Remember, in high school I was trying to fashion myself as an iconoclast. Compared to the well-behaved girls of the Norwood High chorus, we guys in the back row were restless and somewhat difficult to deal with, so in an effort to keep our horseplay from infecting the rest of the chorus, our director, Mr. Dugan, would hand us sheet music and tell us to go into the bathroom and work on it. The boys' room was next door to the music room, so we became the Boys Next Door. We took pride in being sent to the boys' room, in the same way that as youngsters we took pride in being sent to the bench at Shattuck Elementary. As they say, Bad Boys—what are you going to do?

So out of those days of bathroom singing came our quartet. Sponsel was the musician of our group. His real name was Bob but we called him Sponsel because he wore an old wool military coat that said "Lt. Sponsel" on its breast pocket. I'll continue to call him Sponsel so as not to confuse him with my other chum named Bob.

There aren't many guys who were given a full music scholarship to college whose first love is barbershop harmony, but Sponsel was one of them. He was all about the singing and the sheet music. I was the performance guy, I was the attitude, but together we were the heart and pulse of the quartet. I was the Lennon to his McCartney. You can take my comparing us to the Beatles as ridiculous, but I'm going to go ahead and say it's a pretty solid comparison. I had the inexplicable overconfidence that I'd been brimming over with since childhood, and Sponsel was a music snob, and there is no snob like a music snob. We went through various members in high school, finally settling on Sponsel's brother Jim, who played tuba in the band and became the tuba of our quartet. We always had trouble finding someone who could sing the high tenor notes, as all of our voices had changed. Then one day we heard this little underclassman walking down the hallway singing "Message in a Bottle" by the Police, and he was hitting all the notes. We hustled him into the boys' room and made him sing with us. He was tiny and had a voice as sweet as pie, so I called him Squimbo-Pie, and without asking if he was interested, we told him he was part of the group.

A little over a year later we were driving to our new job at Canobie Lake Park in Salem, New Hampshire, in an old 1966 Dodge Dart. It was the same make and model that my dad used to drive. Our bass, Jim, had bought it for a few hundred dollars, and we dubbed it "Harmony Car." With all the singing on the way up, I avoided any carsickness. If only I had known that worked sooner! We pulled into the big empty parking lot and right up to the fence in the shadow of the the Yankee

Cannonball, a big white wooden roller coaster. Canobie Lake was an old-fashioned amusement park on a beautiful piece of land—nothing but big trees, green grass, and all on the shores of a massive lake. There was an old Dancehall Theater on the shore, which from the 1930s to the 1950s had featured big bands like Duke Ellington, Harry James, Jimmy Dorsey, and Frank Sinatra. We had a week of rehearsals ahead of us before the season began in late June. We were introduced to the other performers, who were all professional actors and actresses from New York City. In discussing our new job with them I was surprised to learn that many of them would have preferred to have spent their summers doing "summer stock" or "repertory theater" somewhere besides this theme park. It was likely that this was their third or fourth choice for a summer gig, but that didn't mean they didn't appreciate it. This was a job in "the biz." They were glad to be here instead of waiting tables, and they certainly didn't arrive with any sense of entitlement. We, on the other hand, sure did.

It's hard to describe the combination of naïveté and cockiness that the Boys Next Door had as a group. We were very excited to be working as entertainers—this was our first steady paying gig as a quartet, after all. But we also had a brash attitude as a group that broadcast, Canobie Lake Park were the ones that were "lucky to have us." All I can say is that it's an a cappella thing. You probably remember the look on the faces of the members of your college a cappella group when they got up to sing "unannounced" in the dining hall; the smug expressions that said, "Yeah—we're doing this . . . enjoy!" A cappella singers have no humility at all. That is how we felt about ourselves. Some of this is justified: a cappella music is difficult and takes a long time to master, so when you're starting off, you're terrible at it and very aware of that fact. Once you become proficient, you never stop being proud of yourself. But it's not just the mastery, it's that you're self-contained. You can take it with you. So it gives you the sense that you're welcome anywhere. That doesn't work for other musicians. There are plenty of class-A violin players out there, but you never see them stand up in the middle of a diner and break into "Flight of the Bumblebee."

We got to the park with the sense that we knew what we had to offer, and as card-carrying members of SPEBSQSA, that we didn't have to change to accommodate anyone else's idea of what a barbershop quartet show was supposed to look like. Then we ran headfirst into the park's entertainment director, Mr. G.

Dave Girton was a commanding figure. He was six foot four with shoulder-length bleached blond hair and a copper tan, and had the striking magnetism of a circus lion tamer. He spoke in a deep baritone that commanded attention, and always gestured theatrically. His personality was reminiscent of Gene Wilder's Willy Wonka—he was able to shift from smiling and playful to dark and abusive on a dime. He drove a Porsche with an Indiana vanity plate that read "SHOWBIZ."

From what I could see, Show Biz Inc. was a two-man operation: Mr. G, as everyone called him, and his short, bespectacled assistant, Kenny, the guy we had auditioned for in the hotel ballroom. Because we gave nicknames to everybody, Kenny, owing to his large waist size, became known as Roly Poly-Idioly. It was a dismissive nickname for sure—the man was a professional who was just doing his job—but we looked on him as a toadie to the boss, and we didn't have the same respect for the chain of command that the theater people had. It was Kenny's job to keep us in line while Mr. G concentrated his outsize personality on striking fear into the hearts of his merry band of theatrical players.

All the park entertainers were housed at the out-of-service Pine Valley Motel about twenty-five minutes north of Salem in Hookset, New Hampshire. We were told the motel was used as surplus student housing for the University of New Hampshire, though I found that hard to believe based on the condition of the place. It was a 1960s-style motor lodge—a strip of rooms with doors that opened up to the parking lot. In the middle was a big Swiss chalet–style A-frame building that housed the former office, and an upstairs guest lounge, but the A-frame had been locked up long ago.

We were housed two to a room, and I roomed with Sponsel, our baritone. Jim roomed with his church buddy Brad, and our tenor, Squimbo-Pie was put in with one of the talent supervisors, who ended up functioning as a kind of chaperone for him since he was two years younger than us, and really unprepared to live away from home.

Our salary was $195 a week per singer and because I had done all the talking at the audition, I was considered to be the quartet "spokesman," so would get $210. For that extra money I would be expected to be the point man for the quartet and report to Show Biz Inc. in the event that any one of us had any problems fulfilling our contractual duties.

So there we were, the musical theater folks, Tab Halley the park magician, and the Boys Next Door all crammed together in a run-down, closed motel. Tab was well traveled; he'd performed at theme parks all over the country, and he had developed some strange road-warrior diet habits. One of Tab's specialties was pepperoni pizza with Tums tablets. He would place one Tums atop each pepperoni on the slice, and wolf the whole thing. He claimed to love it. He'd say, "You get used to the taste fairly quickly, and it absolutely kills the heartburn." Tab was in his thirties, which seemed ancient to us, and he wasn't in the best shape, but we had great respect for him because he had tons of experience. He was the real deal, a full-on theatrical magician—the kind of guy I had dreamed of being when I had played around with my magic set as a kid. Tab had a mini-trailer full of amazing illusions that he towed around behind his IROC sports car. He had all the classics: the Interconnecting Rings, the Magic Botania (the trick that has a huge bouquets of flowers appear out of nowhere), the Levitating Woman, the Woman Sawed in Half, and many other things that involved forcing a woman into unnatural positions.

Which is why Tab needed a female assistant. Tab didn't travel with one, as that would have been too costly. He needed a lovely lady supplied by Show Biz Inc. Judy had auditioned for a role in a show, just like all the other New York theater people, but instead was assigned the role of magician's assistant. She wasn't one bit happy about it, and she let it be known. Shortly after we checked in to our motel, she came to our room and introduced herself to us.

"Hi, I'm Judy," she said.

"Hi Judy, we're the Boys Next Door." We stood in our doorway and babbled for a while until she strutted right past us in her NYPD athletic shorts and Adidas running shoes and into our room, sitting down on the corner of one of our beds. Seemingly at home, she told us that the whole reason she had taken the job in the park was so she could do musical theater, and that she never really liked magic. She wanted to sing and dance, not be gawked at while a hula hoop was drawn across her levitating body. She found magic creepy. We nodded our heads sympathetically and said, "I know what you mean," even though we didn't know what she meant at all. We loved magic. But we bonded at our first meeting with Judy, and by *bonded* I mean we listened to her talk and behaved in a charming manner, never once jumping up and down and high-fiving each other over the fact that there was a girl in our hotel room being nice to us.

Later on, when she received her wardrobe, she stormed over, furious. She came to our dressing room to show us the tiny sparkling bikini.

"Can you believe I have to wear this?"

"I can't. That's terrible," I said, "you should probably let them know you don't like it."

Meanwhile I thought it was the greatest costume I had ever seen and I couldn't wait to see her in the live magic show. She was a dancer with amazing legs and I had been barely able to contain myself when she introduced herself in those athletic shorts, never mind this Vegas Showgirl costume.

We told her she should speak up about her concerns, but she assured us it was of no use.

"Mr. G runs this place with an iron fist. You can't challenge him."

"You should think about it," I said. "You have a right to feel comfortable at work."

We all consoled and supported Judy like gentlemen, while we lusted after her in our hearts.

Then it came time for us to go to the costume trailer to pick up our uniforms. We felt Judy's pain right away. The costumes were tuxedo shirts with red ties and cummerbunds and black stretch pants with no pockets—the kind dancers wear. To add insult to injury, we were then given silver vests, with shimmering "eyelash material," which looks like tinsel from a Christmas tree. They were the gayest things I'd ever seen. And I say that in the 1980s-gay way.

"No way."

"There is no way I'm wearing that."

"Uh, uh. No."

"Forget about it."

We were united, and we hadn't even needed to call a quartet conference. All four of us refused to even touch the outfits.

"I'm sorry, Kenny, we're not going to wear those uniforms," I told Idioly.

"Sorry guys, these are the outfits that Mr. G picked out himself. Mr. G doesn't suffer fools gladly. If you want to perform for Show Biz Incorporated, you're gonna have to wear what he picks out for you."

"Then we'll head home right now," I replied.

From his incredulous expression, I could tell that he was not used to performers being willing to walk away from a gig over a costume.

We stood there with dour expressions staring him down in our mismatched tweed vests, probably looking like the Bowery Boys in *Angels with Dirty Faces*, which, to my dad's great disappointment, I've still never seen.

Idioly was shocked. It was clear that he was in over his head. He was dealing with four teenagers who were willing to walk away from a sweet theme park gig because of shiny vests. This didn't happen at Show Business Incorporated! Performers did what they were told!

"Well, we're just gonna have to talk to Mr. G. about this. He's not going to be happy, I'll tell you that."

We walked out of that trailer like Marlon Brando and his buddies in the *Wild Ones,* and went back to our dressing room and made a plan. Late in the afternoon we were summoned to Mr. G's office. He was sitting in a suit and tie in the sparse, refrigerated trailer. Next to him on the wall was a cork board with index cards pinned to it, listing all the shows on a grid organized by locations and times.

He didn't get up. He didn't even look at us. After a dramatic silence he took in a deep breath quickly through his nose and looked up as if he were about to let out an operatic yell, but instead spoke softly: "I understand you boys are refusing to wear the uniforms assigned to you."

I stepped up to speak. I was going to work for that extra fifteen dollars a week. "We can't wear them. They're not appropriate for our style of music." I was hedging because I didn't want to say what I really thought of his outfits.

"They are highly appropriate. Have you heard of vaudeville? I had these designed by the best people in the business. I've been doing shows at parks like this for twenty years."

"We won't wear them. They are not the right style."

"You think you know more than I do about what style is appropriate for this genre? Tell me one thing that is inappropriate about those outfits!"

"They're just not . . . they're not masculine."

Mr. G was taken aback. He looked around at each of us. He knew what I meant. It hadn't occurred to him before, but all of a sudden it made sense. He was from Indiana, after all, a land of farming, jeans, and guys working on tractors. He didn't live in a complete bubble. Perhaps after doing so much musical theater, he had forgotten how the world looked to non-showbiz people. His demeanor quickly changed.

"Okay. All right," he said, nodding his head. "But you're going to have to match. I can't have a quartet walking around in mismatched outfits! It doesn't look professional."

"Understood. We will purchase matching outfits at our own expense," I said, which wasn't a bargaining tactic. I was more than willing to pay so we could wear something we were comfortable with.

"No. No, I'll get them for you. They will be subdued, but genre appropriate. Can you wear these until the new ones arrive?"

"No."

He threw his hands up as if to say, *Who are these dissident harmonizers?*

We hammered out an agreement. We would wear khaki pants with white shirts and matching straight ties in the interim since he had plenty of those in the costume trailer. In two days we would have new uniforms delivered to us via Federal Express—regular black pants with white tuxedo shirts, red bow ties and suspenders, and straw boater hats. To us, it was a classic look—tidy but manly.

When we left Mr. G's trailer we each shook hands with him, and as I was leaving he leaned in to me and spoke softly, "If anyone asks, this was my decision. Tell them I changed my mind on the uniforms after I watched you perform."

"Of course," I said. Mr. G. didn't want the word getting out that he bowed to the will of a performer in any aspect of his shows. He had to maintain his reputation as the director with an iron fist, the all-controlling impresario of premiere theme park entertainment. But I respected him even more, because he knew which battles were worth fighting. Sometimes it's best to leave a headstrong quartet alone.

*

Squimbo-Pie was the Pete Best of the Boys Next Door. (And yes, I'm aware that's the second time I compared my barbershop quartet to the Beatles.) He certainly sang tenor very well, but he never really clicked with the group socially, because of his age. Two years difference seems bigger than it is at that age, and as a result we always treated him like a kid, and it probably led him to behave more like one.

But the night at the park when Squimbo got into the Bartles & Jaymes pretty heavily and threw up all over everybody, he made the decision easy for us. We decided it was time for him to leave. Without consulting anyone at the park we called his mom, and four hours later she was there with the station wagon.

After Squimbo's untimely departure we had to figure out how to proceed. We walked out to our first location in the park and sang a few songs without him—the barbershop trio was a pretty sad-sounding unit, to us anyway, even though it was impressive to hear Sponsel jump effortlessly between baritone and tenor parts throughout the song in order to ring the most chords. To most anyone else listening I'm sure it sounded like classic American songs in perfect harmony, but to us it was just an abomination. We had to do something. We knew if we went to the office, they would probably put us in touch with one of the young show managers. (Mr. G was already gone; he would show up just once more during the summer to "check in" but once the shows were up and running, he left the show in the hands of his young middle-managers.) Their solution would be to find one of the actors from the shows to learn little Squimbo's tenor parts and join our quartet. We didn't want that to happen, though, since we needed to remain an autonomous group. We decided to flee.

Not wanting to be spotted walking out the employee entrance in the middle of the day, we climbed the high fence next to the parking lot in our costumes. Our bosses didn't see us, but we were right out in the open, so some patrons surely did. It may be the only time in history this question was asked aloud: "Honey, is that barbershop trio escaping from an amusement park?"

We piled into Harmony Car and drove off. We got back to Norwood and began our search for a new tenor. We went through anyone who had sung with us in the past. But most of these guys were unable to just uproot themselves in the middle of the summer and join a theme park quartet. Our top choice, Matt Sullivan, from the Norwood High jazz ensemble, was a great musician and loved to sing with us; he was ready to jump at the chance, but his dad wouldn't let him, saying he didn't want his son "horsing around and getting into trouble." Little did he know, other than the occasional Pabst Blue Ribbon, we were as clean living as Mormon missionaries! I'm sure Matt's internship at a Boston PR firm exposed him to far more debauchery than we had to offer him.

We settled on a wild card choice, my old buddy Grover. John Grover was actually Squimbo's cousin. He had never sung in a quartet, but he had a pretty good ear, a fairly pure-sounding falsetto voice, and, most important, he was a lot of fun to be around. The very next morning we were all in the car on our way back to Canobie Lake Park. We showed up for work and expected to be greeted with some type of discipline for walking off the job and missing a day of work, but no one in the office seemed to have even noticed.

The transition from Squimbo to Grover was easy enough: we simply had the name on his checks changed from Jimmy to John, and that was that. The managers were just relieved that we had corrected the problem ourselves so they didn't have to worry about it. We'd kept Squimbo's straw hat, and I lent Grover my spare outfit, which fit him well enough. Grover learned the six easiest songs in our repertoire and never bothered to learn another note. For the rest of the summer he was the happiest and least committed member of the group. In between sets he'd move about the park and socialize. It became obvious pretty quickly that Grover was the Harry Styles of our group—with his longish hair and his boater hat tipped inappropriately back on his head . . . and of course the ladies loved him. He was always going on mini-dates with girls who would separate themselves from their families for the afternoon to take a walk with Grover down by the lake and share a lime rickey. Grover would show up unapologetically late for a set, explaining that he "met a lady." It was amazing to observe.

*

We'd get back from the park at around 8 p.m. At night the culture of the Pine Valley Motel could be described as "off-Broadway in the woods." There was always a full-on party in progress—doors on the musty old motel kept wide open, music drowning out the sound of the crickets and bullfrogs, and a bucket of wine coolers on ice outside. It's hard to fathom, but for about five years in the 1980s wine coolers (containing 0 percent wine and 0 percent cool) were very popular with young people, owing to the durable commercial campaign featuring two old men pretending to be Bartles & Jaymes spouting folksy nonsense, and always ending with "and thank you for your support."

We didn't drink them, though; we preferred Pabst Blue Ribbon, which was not yet a hipster beer, but still the cheapest thing in the store, so it suited us perfectly. None of the guys in the quartet were old enough to buy alcohol, so Tab had to pick up the beer for us, and we'd pick up the pizza. We'd huddle at our end of the motel eating pizza, drinking a couple of PBRs, and singing. No, we were not tired of barbershop singing at the end of the day; we would always be trying out new songs and singing tags.

Tab never tired of our singing, either, so he was the perfect companion. He'd also entertain us with close-up magic while he regaled us with stories of his life in show business. He talked a lot about his glory days at Kings Island, a "real" theme park in Ohio, where they appreciated the kind of classic magic act he provided. Apparently Tab wasn't thrilled with his current gig, although we didn't know why—we couldn't imagine a better summer job. He had complaints about Mr. G, his unappreciative assistant, Judy, and his current pay. He mostly saved his complaints for when he'd had a few too many beers. I think he was glad to have us as buddies for the summer.

Because our barbershop shows were separate from the singing and dancing entertainment, we were often in our own orbit at work. But back at Pine Valley, everyone would mingle together, and, let me tell you, I'd never been around so many gorgeous women. And as far as I could tell, the male actors and dancers didn't seem too interested in them romantically. I thought this might be a bountiful summer for pitching some woo since the odds were clearly in our favor. *How could these ladies resist us—four clean-cut, talented guys who were all but bursting with libidinous energy?*

It seems that they had an easy time of it. We were, perhaps, too "primed." The girls could sense it. Like shaken-up cans of Pabst, they knew if they opened us, we'd overflow. So, most of the girls stayed clear of us, all except Judy, who would talk to us whenever Tab wasn't around. But even with her we were all deep in the friend-zone. She used her time with us to confide in us about her unhappiness as a magician's assistant. And we always listened.

Sometimes I'd talk with a beautiful dancer named Nicole. She was quiet and kept to herself. She seemed grounded and confident. I never saw her drinking wine coolers at night, and she was always up early, sitting in the morning sun behind the motel, doing yoga or meditating, or just stretching.

I'd look out the back window of our room and see her doing her Zen routine. Her curly brown hair was lit by the morning light, and she looked like a stock photo that you'd use for a peaceful greeting card or framed poster that said "Embrace Who You Are" or "Live in the Now . . ."

My morning rite was waking up and looking out the window to see if Nicole was there. We had a little electronic hot pot in our room and I'd make an instant coffee, which I'd enjoy while watching her doing her sun salutations. It may seem like I was acting like a Peeping Tom, but I had only the purest appreciation. To me Nicole was something wholesome. I often thought about going around back and saying hello, but I knew she wouldn't want the interruption—the mornings were her alone time. But if I'd see her at the park on break, I'd say hello, never revealing how much I appreciated her daily ritual. I kept the idea of asking her on a date alive in my mind, but never gathered the courage. Where was the cockiness that I applied to our musical group? It drained away when I saw a pretty face.

*

We used to go to breakfast at Ralph's Place, an old-fashioned silver diner car that was run by a guy named Ralph Spencer. He would sling hash every morning at the grill, while his daughter Gretel ran dishes in and out of the kitchen. We'd line up in a row at the counter and watch Ralph work that grill full of pancakes and eggs, sausage and steaks, and no matter the hour, he had his frosty mug of beer sitting beside him. We'd mostly see Ralph from behind, working furiously as a big sweat stain ran straight down his back, spatula in one hand, reaching for his beer with the other.

Gretel was about twenty-five and very tough, but gorgeous, and as she moved through the diner in a paper-thin T-shirt, she was a sight to behold. When she'd stop by to refill our coffee, we probably looked like four golden retrievers with a biscuit in front of our faces. Every once in a while Ralph would turn his head around quickly to make sure we weren't ogling his daughter, and our heads would snap up, suddenly interested in something on the pegboard menu above the grill. We thought we were subtle, but Ralph was totally on to us.

Once the tin of creamer that was sitting in front of us was empty. I held up the tin and asked, "Could we get some more half and half?"

Ralph drained his beer. "Go get it yourself," he said.

"The half and half?"

"Yeah. Go get it yourself." He opened the refrigerator and cracked open another can of light beer, which he poured into his glass as I sat there holding the tin. "Go in the kitchen and get it yourself."

I got up and walked behind the counter, pushed through the swinging doors into the kitchen. The dishwashers looked up at me and then went back to their work. They had clearly seen this routine before. I looked in a few doors that were filled with produce, and then behind door number three I found my half and half. I flipped up the lid and filled the tin. Then Gretel arrived with a tray full of cream dispensers. "My dad says fill these, too."

Gretel was inches away from me. We stood there for a long moment in front of the open refrigerator, a cloud of cold fog billowing between us. I didn't say anything. She handed me the tray and took the full creamer out of my hand. "I'll take this one," she said, smiling as she turned and pushed through the swinging doors.

I flipped up all the lids and filled them all to the top. Then I backed through the double doors, almost spilling the tray when they swung back in my direction. As I turned around Ralph yelled, "Who needs cream?" and the place erupted in laughter. I then had to walk around and distribute the dispensers.

After that we were regulars at Ralph's, spending more money than we had budgeted on spending for breakfast that summer. But it was worth it for the experience of the place. One day Ralph turned to us and held out a coin.

"I'll flip you for breakfast."

"Free breakfast if we get it?"

"You call the coin. You get it right, breakfast is on me. Wrong, you pay double. Good?"

We lost the toss, and Ralph went back to his grill. We weren't sure if he was serious, but when we got to the register Ralph yelled out to the cashier, "They lost, double or nothing!" and she rung us up twice. He'd obviously done this before, too. But whenever he asked we always took him up on his "I'll flip you for breakfast" offers, winning some and losing some. I'm pretty sure we broke even for the summer.

One morning Tab joined us at the diner. Four clean-cut guys in shorts and polo shirts, and one guy on the end in tux and tails with spandex pants—I'm sure we were a sight. It was the first time we brought Tab to Ralph's Place with us, and he seemed a little preoccupied. When Gretel showed up at the counter to take our order and saw him staring into space, she asked, "Do you need to see a menu?"

"Yes, please."

This was strange. Tab was on the road most of his life, so had probably eaten in hundreds of diners. It seemed odd that he needed to look at a breakfast menu.

When she came back and asked, "You know what you'd like?" Tab pushed the menu back at her and said, "Yeah, two eggs any style with potatoes and toast."

" 'Any' isn't a style."

"What?"

"How do you want your eggs?"

"Scrambled."

When we were all sitting there eating our breakfast, Tab got up and wandered like a zombie out into the foyer of the diner where the real estate magazines and bubble gum machines were. He clearly had something on his mind. Then, very suddenly, pushed open the door and ran down the stairs. He darted across the parking lot, tuxedo tails flying behind him, jumped into his IROC sports car, and screeched out of the parking lot. His magic trailer swung back and forth violently as he turned onto Route 24 and peeled away.

Ralph turned to us with a look that said, *Somebody's paying for that guy's breakfast.*

We flipped Ralph for it of course, and lost, so we ended up having to pay for ten breakfasts. On our way to the park we discussed Tab's odd exit. Was it a dine and dash, with the joke on us? Tab was known for pranks, if you could believe his stories about his old days on the magic circuit. But just running out on a check didn't seem to be Tab's style. There was no flair. It was just weird.

We got to the employee parking lot and punched the clock, then walked to our dressing room the long way so we could pass by Tab's magic hut. He was on the platform behind the hut, sitting on a trunk and staring into his hat, tears running down his face. Tab had fallen into the magic abyss.

"What's up, Tab?" Sponsel asked.

He didn't answer. We walked up onto the platform and crowded around him. As we got close we could see down into the top hat. At the bottom were Tab's three white doves he used for his miraculous final trick.

This was the trick when his birds flew into the top hat, which he then flipped up to show to the audience . . . and poof the birds were gone! On the applause, he clapped the top of the hat which folded up as flat as a pancake, and took a bow. He then walked off stage, leaving the hat backstage when he came out for his encore bow, but after the show he always returned to tend to his birds, which were crushed into the flat hat. That's the trick! The trick is there is no trick—it's a matter of crushing birds into the bottom of a hat. White doves possess a very special quality—they don't complain when they are squeezed into small spaces. In fact, they feel very content and secure in there. That's why magicians love them so much; they are very willing to be stuck into tiny folds of material, where they will remain, silently waiting to be released. But you must actually release them. Otherwise they will suffocate. They only have a few minutes of air, so the first thing a magician does after the show is release his birds from their cramped prisons and put them back into their cages. Tab had forgotten to do that the night before. And, now, he was crushed.

I felt bad for Tab and tried to convince him that it was a mistake that any magician could make. He was rather inconsolable—he felt that he had broken a kind of magician's code.

I'm not sure what had made him forget his birds that night. Tab was a little disheveled with his uniform, and had sloppy eating habits, but he had always been a careful magician. He was very good at what he did. I wondered if this was going to be Tab's last theme park. He talked about his old gigs at Kings Island as if his glory days had passed him by. I still admired him, and I wished he could be enjoying this summer job as much as I was. To me this was magic. Being in an amusement park all day with my friends, and being paid to sing songs.

*

The end of the summer was approaching. Our final show of each day was at 7 p.m. aboard the *Canobie Queen*, a sunset cruise as the days got shorter.

One night after the last show I was stepping off the dock and spotted Nicole walking up the hill, so I ran to catch up with her. I don't know what came over me, but I just blurted out, "Do you want to get a coffee sometime?"

"Oh, that's very nice," she said. "But I'm leaving in three days. I have to go to school. I'm going to Syracuse University and I have to start early."

"Oh, that's great. You must be excited."

"I'm very excited. I'll be sad to leave, it has been a great summer."

It had been a great summer—not just because of all the fun we had, but the world it had opened up for me. Working with people who were living their dreams, even if they weren't necessarily achieving what they thought were their wildest dreams.

I walked her back to the employee entrance. We made small talk and the conversation flowed easily. In many instances, postrejection is the perfect time to talk to a girl because all of the tension is gone.

That twilight walk across the tree-lined park was one of the finer moments of the summer.

The circumstances that led to that summer job had come about because I'd had what many would think was a silly idea—that I could use my barbershop quartet as a way to gain mainstream fame and break into television. Like most of the good things I've achieved in my life, by applying a strange combination of naïveté and hubris, I didn't achieve what I set out to do, but then, undeterred, I tried the next best thing. I got a job, I had an experience, I learned, and I grew. So, maybe the original idea wasn't so silly.

CHAPTER 22

BE PROUD

IT IS FEBRUARY 17, 2014, AND I AM THERE IN STUDIO 6B AT 30 Rock on the evening of the debut episode of *The Tonight Show Starring Jimmy Fallon*. Bono and U2 are on the roof of the building doing a song to close the show, and I am standing there in my straw hat watching them on the monitor. I am there on opening night to rehearse a song with Jimmy and his Rag Time Gals barbershop quartet for the following night's show. We were called in to rehearse the song in front of *The Tonight Show*'s executive producer, Lorne Michaels. We sing for him as he smiles and nods his head. I don't tell him that twenty-five years before I had mailed him a VHS tape of myself singing barbershop in the hopes of getting on *SNL*. Remember when I said some stories have unexpected endings?

Now I make regular appearances on *The Tonight Show* singing with the most well-known barbershop quartet in history.

The Rag Time Gals have performed with Justin Timberlake, Kevin Spacey, Steve Carrel, and Sting. Our videos have been watched 50 million times on YouTube.

Where I am in my life right now, and why I've jumped ahead twenty-five years in my story, is the same reason that I decided to write this book. When I think of the wonderful aspects of my life now—my family, my career, everything that brings me happiness—they are all a result of the things I learned in my early years.

I've turned my old-fashioned upbringing into a career. Of course, I spent a long time trying to break into show business by twisting myself into whatever I thought the entertainment industry wanted or needed. Those years were frustrating, and there were a lot of false starts after my stint in the theme park. I had a lot of really bad, sad, and lame jobs. But then I settled on doing what I do best, and the industry eventually caught up to me. Or, I guess when I started doing what I do best is when the industry realized that I had something to offer.

Nothing really happened for me until I got married. It was the love of a great woman, and the responsibility of raising children, that gave me the focus I needed to put my career into motion, for real. I had been working in show business as a comedian, but not really with any kind of momentum until I had a family. It was that change in my life that changed everything for me.

I'm always telling stories. If I'm working out a family issue with my daughters, I usually start with a story from my childhood. I must be good at it because at bedtime my daughters always say, "Dad, tell us a story from when you were a kid!" The fact that they are fast asleep within three minutes means I'm really boring or a genius. I once fell asleep during the Royal

Shakespeare Company production of *Hamlet,* so I'm going to go with genius.

Gradually, in front of audiences all over the country, I began to use my stories as the framework for the material in my stand-up act. It worked. People started to respond to my brand of humor—jokes that were spun out of nostalgic stories, PG-rated at most, and rooted in core values of family, respect, and patriotism. I spent several years touring the country performing my decidedly clean comedy act. I was opening act for the "King of Clean Comedy" himself, Jim Gaffigan, and got to perform for theaters full of Americans of all ages, in forty-six of the fifty states. Sometimes the tours were a fun-for-the-whole-family experience. During the summer months I would take my family along with me, and Jim and his wife, Jeannie, would bring their five kids along, too. The eleven of us were a sight to behold at the hotel pool. One Thanksgiving we were in Las Vegas and Jim and Jeannie treated us all to a performance of the *Tournament of Kings* at the Excalibur hotel, the "show and dinner experience of Medieval proportions." There we were, Eleven Lords and Ladies eating eleven chickens, screaming at the top of our lungs as our appointed knights battled with jousts and swords. I felt so lucky to be with my family and my friends, doing the thing that I wanted to do for a living since I was a teenager.

Those tours were such a blast, but I had to leave it all behind for the chance of a lifetime when I was given the opportunity to host my own nightly show on the Fox News Channel. That was something I never expected—being on television almost every night with a massive audience (Fox News has one of the biggest audiences in all of television) and being allowed to offer my fresh yet distinctly traditional take on the political issues of the day. Five days a week on *Red Eye with Tom Shillue*, I performed monologues with titles like "We don't need successful kids, we need happy ones" and "Is less now more in today's world?" and "Good parents are willing to wait a few decades for a 'Thanks Dad!'" Now, where do you think I got the ideas for those? My job at Fox puts me in front of millions of eyeballs, where I often spout the ideas of my dear old dad, William T. Shillue, and the notions I heard time and time again years ago in Norwood, Massachusetts.

Raising a family in New York City is much different than how I grew up, but I do my best to try and bring a little of what I had to my kids' lives. Our Riverdale neighborhood in the Bronx has lots of outdoor spaces, parks, and ball fields. I, like most of the parents in the area, enjoy taking the kids out to the park. We just let them go. We keep watch over them, for sure, but try not to hover. Instead of being a helicopter parent, the trend of the day, I try to be more of a golf-cart security guard, circling the perimeter but staying out of the way. We let them go a little way into the woods to explore and pretend, and to play games without any interference or assistance. Sometimes if there's a little rumble, the kids run to the adults to intercede. I always send mine on their way. "Work it out!" I yell. That's my favorite phrase. I'm famous for it in the neighborhood—"Oh, boy, here comes the work-it-out-guy," I hear, but I will continue saying it. My parents never had to say it to me, because they were never around for any of the rumbles. Running to them to intervene in every little argument wasn't even an option.

Sometimes when the kids are out of sight but not earshot, I can tell from their conversations that they think we adults can't hear them and they are saying things they shouldn't be saying. Sometimes the other kids are not being nice to my kids, and sometimes my kids are the ones being mean. I stay out of it. Most of my childhood was spent in the middle of these name-calling battles. I learned to work things out. In these ways, and with my stories, I try to teach my kids the same values that I learned as a kid.

When I see my kids embodying my old-fashioned ideals, I beam with pride. One wet, overcast day when my daughter Agnes was five, I took her down to the nearby park to play. Because of the weather that day, there was only a little boy and his dad there with us. As our kids started playing together, we dads started checking our iPhones. (I am always telling my kids to "go play together" and "don't be shy," but when it comes to other dads, I don't really follow my own advice.)

At some point I heard my daughter say "Bang!" and I looked up to see her pointing at the little boy from behind the slide. Then the little boy pointed at Agnes from behind the monkey bars. "Bang!" he said back. Then she scooted to the side, spun around, and pointed again, "Bang." He returned fire, "Bang! Bang!"

The other dad jerked his head up so quickly, he almost dropped his phone. He took off running toward the monkey bars yelling, "Dean . . . No! No guns!" The boy dropped his arms to his side, and the father bent down to address his son. "I've told you," he said softly, "no guns."

My daughter walked right up to the dad with her hand still in the shape of a gun, and held it out to him. "It's not real," she said. Then she flipped her hand back and forth to show both sides. "See? It's not real."

The dad looked up at me, perhaps hoping I would get involved, and I just arched my eyebrows and shrugged as if to say, "Makes total sense to me." My daughter had done exactly what I would have done as a kid and something that just plain makes sense.

Of course if I parented *exactly* like my own parents, Child Services would probably come a-knocking. So, in order to avoid being judged by the touchy-feely modern parents in the neighborhood, I've learned to speak their language when necessary. Sometimes, however, the patented Shillue style seeps out. Once my daughter Louise was acting up on the playground, as kids do, and making excuses for her behavior. She was screaming about how bad she felt about something or other to keep me from getting angry.

"I don't care how you feel, I care how you behave," I said. It must have sounded harsh because it caught the attention of the mom next to me on the playground. Louise walked away, not entirely content with the situation, but behaving better.

"What did you just say?" the mom asked me.

I said, "I don't care how you feel, I care how you behave."

"Where'd you get that one?" she asked.

"I'm pretty sure my mother used to say it."

The mother seemed a little unsettled, but also a little intrigued. I think she might have put it into her repertoire.

Of course, I do care about what my daughter is feeling. I just want her to know that feelings don't come first. Behavior is first, then feelings second. Most of the parents on the playground have it the other way around. Obviously, as a parent I need to strike a balance, a happy medium—go along with the rest of the world, but offer some resistance. And of course, always keep my mom's aphorisms in my holster, at the ready.

Here's the thing. I'm proud of how I'm raising my kids.

I'm proud of what I'm able to do with my career now, and how my beliefs and values have helped give me that career. Some of the things may sound old-fashioned or out of step, but they work. They helped me grow up to be content and give something to the world. If I can do that for my kids, all the better.

CHAPTER 23

BE GRATEFUL

MY UNCLE BOBBY WAS ALWAYS THE COOL UNCLE. When he'd come to visit us with my grandmother when I was a kid, we'd ride bikes together around the neighborhood. On Christmas morning he liked to play with our toys right alongside us. He seemed as excited about the train sets as we were. Bobby wasn't like the other grown-ups. He was fun. He didn't yell. He was easy to be around.

One day when Bobby was visiting, we were out riding bikes together, and I heard my dad discussing Bobby with our neighbor, Mr. Sullivan. As he was raking his yard, he yelled over to my dad.

"Hey what's wrong with him anyway? Is he just slow?"

"Yeah, he's a little slow," my dad answered.

What were they talking about, slow? Why, because of the bicycle? Bobby is cool!

I rejected whatever my dad and Mr. Sullivan had to say about my uncle. That is, until a few years later, when we started getting more grown-up gifts for Christmas. Bobby didn't get so excited about those. That's when we began to reassess our uncle.

Gradually we came to realize that Uncle Bobby, my mom's youngest brother, was slow. Or as my family called him, retarded. The word was not a slur then. Not even when it was deliberately being used as a slur. "What are you, retarded?" was a pretty innocuous comment; it just meant "Hey—what's wrong with you?"

*

I was going to spend my second year of college at UMASS Boston; the state school was, for Massachusetts residents, about the biggest educational bargain there was. Tuition was a whopping $750 (yes, that's seven hundred and fifty dollars) per semester. I applied for and received a $3,000 loan for the year, so when I went to pay my tuition I actually got cash back, but that was promptly eaten up by books, my meal plan, and various other expenses. I was at a zero balance, so my mother had the idea that I should move in with my grandmother in Dorchester, on the edge of Boston. She lived in the St. Gregory's parish (in Dorchester your parish is your neighborhood), which was the last stop on the T at the Ashmont Station, on the MBTA Red Line. That way I could be in the city and take the subway to school.

"It's perfect," she said. "My room is still there, just as I left it. Nothing's changed."

So I moved in with my grandmother, and my uncle Bobby.

The house was just as it was when I visited on the holidays, decorated in standard Old Lady Catholic: small, dark rooms with multiple oriental carpets and religious portraits covering the walls. There were glass bowls on the glass tables filled with gumdrops. Lace pillows and afghans on the sofas, old-lady smell everywhere. The presence of a fifty-two-year-old son who had never left home was the only departure from the perfectly typical.

My grandmother didn't move quickly but was in constant motion. There was always work to be done, accompanied by her endless stream of patented catchphrases. She would vacuum the oriental rugs while repeating over and over, "The only thing that ever aged a rug is dirt!" or, apparently in reference to nothing, "Money makes money!" What she meant by this I never knew. Also there was lots of talk regarding potatoes. If she were on the phone in the afternoon, she would often excuse herself abruptly. "I gotta go put on my potatoes—good-bye!" That water had to be boiling by 4 p.m. sharp.

Although she was constantly working, neither Bobby nor I ever did anything to help; she wouldn't allow it. This was woman's work, and if I offered any assistance, I was met with a curt, "Be useful and get out of my way!"

My grandmother, like most biscuit-making, kindly little old ladies, spent a lot of her time yelling. She'd stand at the window and yell in the direction of the tough teens outside on the corner of Dorchester Avenue, "Go home to your own neighborhood!" She didn't care that nobody heard her.

"Oh, yeah . . . that's right . . . home to your own neighborhood . . ." Uncle Bobby would echo from his easy chair. Okay, maybe one person heard.

And despite her work ethic, and the fact that she always

exercised her right to vote and drive well over the speed limit, no one could accuse my grandmother of radical feminism. She and Bobby would be sitting in front of the TV when I came home in the early evening. Liz Walker, the local NBC anchorwoman, would be reading the news.

"Get back to your kitchen!" she would yell at the screen.

I remember specifically that phrase—it wasn't "Why don't you go on home and make dinner!" or "You should be at home in the kitchen!" but rather, *"Get back to your kitchen!"* As if there really was a kitchen, perhaps just out of sight behind the TV news set, in which a roast was turning to charcoal and potatoes were boiling over, victims of Liz Walker's ruthless career ambition.

"That's right . . . back to your kitchen," Bobby would parrot.

Bobby never had any original thoughts—only the thoughts of my grandmother, which he would dutifully and enthusiastically repeat back to her. I know that this was simply Bobby's way—I tried not to hold it against him—but sometimes I got the feeling that it was two-against-one. You know when there are three roommates, and one always ends up the odd man out? That was me. I was the third wheel. The uncool roommate. My grandmother and Uncle Bobby would team up on me constantly.

I had to sleep in my mother's old room, in her old bed. The room was largely as she had left it the day she left home to start her own family. A twin bed, Rosary beads over the bedpost, a dresser with a round mirror, with a picture of Jesus above it. Not the kind-looking Jesus handing out loaves and fish—no, the intimidating Jesus who was looking at you out of the top of his eyes with a stern expression as he was opening his chest to expose a thorn-rimmed heart. I would come in late at night and turn on the dim lamp, and he would be staring at me with an expression that said, "Is there something you're not telling me?"

My grandmother did not believe in waking up to buzzers or bells. "Say a prayer and God will wake you up!" That was her method: when you prayed at night, you were to simply mention what time you wanted to wake up in the morning, and God would wake you up at the exact appointed time. Amazingly, this method worked—for my grandmother and my uncle. At 6:15 every morning without fail, they would simultaneously rise from their beds like synchronized swimmers from the spectral plane, and step noiselessly into their slippers to begin their day. I would usually oversleep. *Was my wake-up call being ignored? Or was I not putting enough effort into the non-wake-up-call part of the evening prayers?* That was very possible. Or was God's wake-up alarm some kind of New Age sound—a pan-flute solo, or a cascading flourish on the hammered dulcimer? Because I think I would sleep right through that.

My grandmother also insisted that all inside doors remain open at all times. She didn't say why. I don't believe it was for safety; I know for a fact that in the case of a fire in the home, a closed door is best. But I suspect that my grandmother was more concerned that a closed door might lead to something else, something that would in turn lead to a fire of a different kind.

In a loose interpretation of the door rule, I was allowed to keep my bedroom door slightly ajar when I went to sleep. After the inevitable oversleeping, my grandmother would then wake me up using this curious method: she would reach through the crack, and bring her arm around to bang repeatedly on the back of the door with the palm of her hand. I would awake in a fog to this loud drumbeat and then, looking to my left, I would see an elderly, disembodied arm flapping against the door. It was spine-chilling. But it woke me up.

The house thrived on routine. Wheat flakes with sliced bananas would be waiting on the table in the morning. As I sat down, my grandmother would pour the milk over the flakes, then wipe butter on my toast and then pour boiling water over a tablespoon of Sanka. I didn't have to do anything for myself. I remember thinking, *This is the way Bobby lives his whole life.* Everything was set in a constant, familiar pattern. After breakfast, Bobby would change into his dark-green janitor's uniform that had been left out by his mother, folded neatly on the chair in his bedroom, take his bag lunch and two subway tokens from the telephone table at the bottom of the stairs, and go off to work at the Prudential Center. He swept floors and emptied trash bins five days a week, year after year, and his paycheck was always deposited directly into his savings account. He never spent a dime of his pay; he never had to.

Bobby probably enjoyed his job, and I imagine he was treated well—certainly better than he had been in school. Years ago when Bobby was in school there were no special needs classes, nothing tailored to those who were learning impaired. Kids like Bobby just went to regular school and were labeled "slow." The nuns, with only rulers for discipline, were probably not keen on "child-centered learning," so he was just the dumb kid who happened to come home every day with sore knuckles. My mom told me he had a tough time in school, but he never complained—he was not the complaining type, unless it was to repeat a complaint his mother made. I'm sure he just got

through every day of school as best he could, and then went
home to his mother every night, who made him dinner and
tucked him into bed. One thing he was good at was his prayers.
He knew them all. And he loved the Mass. Bobby could recite
the entire Catholic Mass in Latin. He would do it at home in
front of the fireplace.

Meanwhile, I settled into my college student routine. When
I came home late at night, I would let myself in the front door
with my keys. It was an old door with old locks that would
stick—some nights I would spend several minutes out in the
cold trying to get those old tumblers to fall into place so the key
would turn. I approached my grandmother with the problem.

"Don't force it!" she said. "Just jiggle it. It will open if you
jiggle it!"

"That's right, Tommy. Don't force it."

Thanks, Bobby.

I got home late one frigid night and my key would once
again not turn. I stood outside for some time jiggling. Nothing. I jiggled some more. It was about 22 degrees. Finally I got
impatient, gave a hard and quick turn to the key. It broke off
cleanly.

I stood in the cold for a few minutes, and then, realizing I
had few options, took the metal knocker and knocked on the
door. *Tap, Tap, Tap.* I waited. *Tap, Tap, Tap.*

A minute later I saw Bobby's figure at the top of the stairs
pause, and then begin walking down slowly with his pajamas
buttoned to the top. I had interrupted his extremely consistent
sleep schedule, ordained by God. *Is that a smile? Is he smiling?* I
wondered. *He doesn't know how to smirk, does he?* It looked like a
smirk.

The door opened. Bobby looked at me blankly, and then

down to the lock, and then slowly back up to me. I swear I could see a smirk.

"You forced it, Tommy." He wanted to make sure he could savor the moment.

"You shouldn't have forced it, Tommy." He kept his hand on the door.

There I was. Alone with Bobby—I would have thought that when it came down to the two of us, man to man, I would have had the upper hand. But it was Bobby for the win. I was on his turf, and he knew it. I had been told not to force it, but I did it anyway. And now I was standing on a concrete porch in freezing cold at one in the morning being upbraided by the slow guy.

*

A few years later, when I was living in New York and sharing an apartment with my sister Ann, my grandmother died. We drove back to Boston for the funeral. In addition to my mother, my grandmother had three sons, but they all decided I should give a eulogy at the service, owing to my experience as a "public speaker." Of course, I am more than comfortable getting up in front of crowds and speaking as a comedian, but this was different. This was my family, and someone very important to us had just died. I don't have a lot of icebreakers for this kind of audience, and my copy of *Doc Blakely's Handbook of Wit and Pungent Humor* was back on my bookshelf in New York.

I was used to standing on altars. I'd been an altar boy, for goodness sake, and had served at many funerals and many weddings. But up on this altar, I was nervous. It was the crowd, the way they stared blankly at me. It is often said of a great performer, "He really knows his audience," but I couldn't possibly know a crowd better than my own family, and yet these guys looked unforgiving.

"Margaret Corrigan . . ." I began.

Why am I calling my grandmother by her first name? It seems wrong, but I can't call her what I normally call her, "Nanny," in church. Can I? And with the body right there in front of me, shouldn't I use her full name?

I went on: ". . . there were many people here that meant so much to Margaret—like Richard, Jackie, Rosemary . . ."

Hey, that's my mother. Rosemary is my mother's name. It is absolutely inappropriate to call your mother by her first name, isn't it? But I'm already committed to the first-name thing so I've got to stick with it. I've only been up here for ninety seconds, how am I supposed to fill five minutes?

I droned on for a few minutes, and I ended by saying, "Thank you for coming . . . God bless you." I looked over my shoulder at the priest, who was giving me a look like, *You didn't say God bless you, did you? You can't say that; that's what I say.*

Was he right? Do I not get to say that? And was I right about what the priest was thinking as he looked at me? Why can't I say it? Don't people say God bless you every time someone sneezes? Maybe you're allowed to say it anywhere except church.

I slid back to my seat. I'm not sure what happened for the rest of the service. The only thing I can be sure of is that my grandmother didn't sit up and critique my performance. But I was sure everyone else had.

At the afterwake, which is when Catholic families have sandwiches, I was feeling insecure about my eulogy. It didn't seem to have gone too well, since no one was saying anything about it. But while everyone was standing around eating their chicken salad and deviled ham, I could see my uncle Bobby pushing through the crowd, making a beeline to me. He stuck out his big, thick hand to me, and I shook his hand. "Tommy, that was a very thoughtful speech you gave. Thank you."

That put me at ease. Then I realized that this was the first time I had ever heard Bobby utter an original thought. I couldn't believe it. Bobby only parroted things his mother said. Then he walked away from me, walked right up to my sister and said, "Ann, thank you for coming, and driving a long way. Please, have a sandwich." Another original thought. I had never heard anything like this from Bobby before. He was taking the initiative.

I realized Bobby had just been waiting for his moment, so he could do a little thinking for himself. And that unfortunate moment happened to be his mother's death. She had always done everything for him. She made his breakfast in the morning. She left his tokens out on the banister. She set up his dinner on a TV tray when he came home from work. Now that she was dead, he was going to have to get smart, or who knows what would happen.

If anyone in that room was worried about how Bobby was going to take care of himself, his actions were telling them, "I'm okay. You don't have to put me in a home. Bobby's fine."

So it didn't take long for everyone to realize that Bobby *was* going to be fine living on his own in Dorchester. He took over the house, and owned it outright. Financially, he was more than sound—all those janitor paychecks that he never spent? My grandmother put them directly into the market, in America's top dividend-paying companies. Did you ever wonder what would happen if you put every paycheck you earned into stocks? Wealth is what would happen.

As an independent adult, Bobby's days were a whirlwind of activity. Instead of his bag lunch from Mom, he went up to the Carney Hospital refectory for lunch. He started singing in the St. Gregory's choir—or at least he moved his lips. He even went to AA meetings once a week. He never had a drink in his life; he just went for the free coffee and conversation.

*

After twenty years in the house in Dorchester on his own, my uncle Bobby passed away. He had been alone in the old house, but he had frequent visitors—his brothers and sisters, and his neighbors. He went to church a lot. I took my wife and children back to Boston for the wake and the funeral. The night we arrived, we checked into a hotel and had dinner with my parents. That's when I told them I was working on this book.

"What kind of book?" my dad asked.

"Stories. Stuff from my life—it's mostly about growing up."

"Sounds interesting," he said. "Am I in it?"

"I imagine you're probably going to make an appearance or two," I answered.

"I would imagine so, yes. I can't wait to read it."

Conversations with my dad have always been like this. Short and staccato. Like years ago when he was telling me to "smile at 'em," or painfully reading the lyric sheet to Meat Loaf's "Paradise by the Dashboard Light." But now they're a lot more comfortable. Now I can read more in between the lines. The awkward pauses are not so awkward anymore.

My mother then told me that some of her siblings had spoken and, once again, they'd like me to give the eulogy. I said I'd be more than happy to, but when we got back to the hotel,

I started fretting over it. I wondered if I should discuss Bobby's disability—whether there was a tactful way to approach it. Should I talk about my time living with him? That he had a propensity for bullying me with the old lady? I knew I could get a laugh with the "don't force it" story, but I wasn't sure what the larger point was supposed to be. Like most of my stories, that one was about me, and what I was going through at the time. I needed to talk about Bobby.

I decided I wouldn't tell the broken-key story, I would avoid any talk of disabilities, and I would give a generic speech full of clichés about life and death. It may not be profound, but it would be safe, and at least my kids, who weren't familiar with any of the clichés, would think I was a great philosopher.

The next day my dad walked up to me in the lobby of the funeral home, and said, "You're off the hook. I'm doing it."

I felt an immediate sense of relief. My dad was good at these things. The man shines at funerals. He's not a natural performer like me—he's probably only spoken in front of a crowd a handful of times, but every time there was a casket in the room. As we walked into the church, he said to me, "Do me a favor, keep an eye on me up there."

I took this to mean, "You, son, are the professional . . . keep an eye on me up there, let me know how I do." When the time came, the priest called him up to the altar, and my father pulled a sheet of paper out of his breast pocket and smoothed it out on the lectern. I sat and watched him work. He spoke slowly, with long pauses, but with great command of his audience.

He began: "A child's problems are often a test of the parents. In that sense we are here to celebrate the loving obstinacy of John and Margaret Corrigan. It was they who came together with courage in the face of the incredibly painful realization that their youngest was, in the world's eye, defective . . ."

The word "defective" echoed through the church. My dad was obviously not one to shy away from the whole "disability" issue. He went on to praise Bobby's innocence and piety, his value as a person, despite his disability. And yes, on earth, *he was defective*, but where he was going none of that mattered, and when we die, we could only hope to have a soul as pure as his.

My dad touched on everything . . . the sacred, the secular; it was masterful. And concluded with this: "On the final day, the day of judgment . . . when the great and mighty and the glib and the shamed stand mute in fear, Bobby will shatter the silence with these words: 'I always did what my mother told me.' "

Eyes welled from the Shillue side of the family. Tears flowed from the Corrigan side. Handkerchiefs came out. My dad was good. He stepped down off the altar, genuflected, slipped into the pew, and stared straight ahead for the rest of the Mass.

Afterward I was in the parking lot putting my key in the rental car ignition, and I saw him walking toward me. I was thinking of what I was going to say to him when he asked me how he had done. Should I tell him he's a master? The best there is? That I could have never done half as well? Or should I just say "Not bad, Dad!" and leave it at that?

When he got to me, he reached into his breast pocket, pulled out the folded speech, pointed it directly at my face, and said: "Put *that* in your book."

So I did.

I started this book with an image of my father as I saw him as a child, and I end this book with an image of my father, the same man, but as I see him now in sharper relief. The stories in between are meant to illustrate how my life is better for the great American values that I was fortunate enough to be raised with.

Today, these values can be seen by many as out of step with the times, corny, unrealistic, and unpopular. But guess what? They work. They make you happy, they make you successful, and, most important, they make you grateful. And the gifts they bring are enormous, so it would be a mistake for me not to pass them on.

I learned so much because of the way I was raised.

From my dad I learned respect for family, tradition, and God. And as I watched him from my perch at my bedroom window at night, I learned to appreciate the wisdom of silence. I absorbed his respect for authority, albeit with his healthy dose of skepticism and a fierce streak of individualism. He also prepared me for The Bastards, with whom I've had more than a few run-ins during my adult years.

From my mom I learned how to take care of myself, and how to be creative and find solutions to life's problems. And I retained her love of art and entrepreneurship. And on our long drives together, a love of theology.

From my brother and sisters, I learned more than I care to admit. They were also my first audience, as I spent my early years trying to make them laugh. I think growing up in a big family confers the kind of generous rewards that can't be expressed in statistics. I remember when my brother spoke as my best man at my wedding, he finished by turning to me and saying, "I've got your back." That's it. We may not get together that often these days, but as siblings we always know we've got one another's backs.

From my neighborhood I learned survival skills and a healthy love of competition. Whether from the friends or the so-called bullies, they all played their part. I grew up with a little bit of rough and tumble, and a whole lot of fun and independence.

And I learned from the institutions that helped shape me. From the Church I learned reverence and humility; from the Scouts I gained a love of the outdoors and the will to Be Prepared.

So that when I reached those awkward teenage years, full of soul-searching and rebelliousness, I had a foundation to keep me (somewhat) grounded. And when it came time to start a family of my own, I could return to that foundation, and discover just how strong it had remained.

I feel lucky. And grateful.

ACKNOWLEDGMENTS

Outside of my family, I want to thank these people for helping me with this book: Kelly Van Valkenberg, Anthony Matteo, Josh Sandler, and Olivia Wingate, who believed I had a book in me and helped me to pitch it. Everyone at Dey Street, including Lynn Grady, Michael Barrs, Heidi Richter, Jeanne Reina, Nyamekye Waliyaya, Julia Meltzer, and especially my amazing editor Carrie Thornton, who made me work so hard I'm considering pitching a second book called *Mean Editors for a Better America*. I want to thank Suzanne Scott and Bill Shine at Fox News, and all my great colleagues at FNC, especially Greg Gutfeld and Dana Perino. Also Jim and Jeannie Gaffigan, who I'd still be working for if I didn't have this great TV gig. And of course, Aaron Guild, who left his plow to fight in the war. (Everyone from Norwood will get that last one.)

ABOUT THE AUTHOR

Tom Shillue is a popular host on Fox News Channel. He has appeared in his own *Comedy Central Special*, on *Late Night with Conan O'Brien*, *Last Comic Standing*, *Comics Unleashed*, *Broad City*, and in the feature film *Mystery Team*. Shillue has been featured as part of the barbershop quartet on *The Tonight Show with Jimmy Fallon* along with Justin Timberlake, Kevin Spacey, Steve Carrel, and Sting. In 2013 Shillue released twelve consecutive comedy albums as part of his ambitious "12 in 12" project. From 2012 to 2015, he toured the U.S.A. with friend and fellow comedian Jim Gaffigan. In 2014 he brought his solo show "Impossible" to the Edinburgh Fringe Festival and in 2016 he headlined at SF Sketchfest in San Francisco. He lives in New York City.